Celebration of
Miracles

Celebration of Miracles

JODIE BERNDT

Guideposts®

CARMEL • NEW YORK 10512

This Guideposts edition is published by special arrangement with Thomas Nelson Publishers.

Unless otherwise noted, Scripture references are from THE NEW KING JAMES VERSION. Copyright © 1979, 1980, 1982 Thomas Nelson, Inc., Publishers.

Scriptures indicated NIV are from The Holy Bible: NEW INTERNATIONAL VERSION. Copyright © 1978 by the New York International Bible Society.
Used by permission of Zondervan Bible Publishers.

Library of Congress Cataloging-in-Publication Data
Berndt, Jodie.
Celebration of miracles : an intriguing look at miraculous events
that touch our lives / Jodie Berndt.
p.   cm.
Includes bibliographical references.
ISBN 0-7852-7690-4
1. Miracles—Case studies. I. Title.
BT97.2.B47 1995
231.7'3—dc20 95-32409
CIP

Designed by José R. Fonfrias

Printed in the United States of America.

This book is dedicated to
Hillary, Annesley, and Virginia Jane…

and, with love and gratitude, to their father, Robbie…

and to the glory of our heavenly Father,
who still makes miracles happen.

Contents

Contents

~ *Acknowledgments* ~

WHEN I BEGAN WRITING THIS BOOK, the folks at Thomas Nelson were clear about what they wanted: *Celebration of Miracles*, they said, should be the kind of book a reader could "dip into" at any point and come away encouraged and inspired.

The stories in this book have certainly been an inspiration to me—yet they took me beyond my expectations. In studying and retelling the miracles, I felt the raw, energetic, and compelling power of God in a way I had never before witnessed or experienced. For giving me this privilege, I am grateful to each of the people whose stories appear on these pages. Thank you for opening your lives so that others may see and know God's incredible love.

I also want to acknowledge and thank the many friends who offered prayers and other tangible demonstrations of support during this project, including Ron and Judy Blue, Jim and Anne Ryun, Zoe Custer, Fran LaMattina, Gary and Anne Gaddini, Shade and Maria Honeycutt, and Margaret Hamilton. Thanks, too, to Cynthia Giddens, Jenny Wamsley, and Kate Kemether for sharing love and attention with my children while I raced to meet deadlines, and to Dr. Joe Woods and Dr. Jon York for patiently fielding my questions as I attempted to verify medical problems and translate complex doctor jargon into plain, readable English.

Next, I am indebted to the outstanding team at Thomas Nelson—especially Esther Fitzpatrick, who helped coordinate all the elements in this book and keep us on track, and Lisa Moyers, who turned a few slim leads into a stack of timely and valuable research. I am also grateful for Sue Ann Jones, whose special blend of editing expertise and cheerful enthusiasm makes correction so easy to take.

Most of all, I appreciate my editor, Janet Thoma, who imposed deadlines with grace, pushed with encouragement, and turned the vision for *Celebration of Miracles* into an exciting reality.

Finally, I thank God for my family: my parents, Allen and Claire Rundle, who taught me to believe in the God of miracles; my husband, Robbie, who provided the spiritual, physical, and emotional support and love I needed to undertake this project; and our precious daughters, who gave me endless grace and whose faithful, tender prayers enabled me to approach my work with joy.

A note to the reader: Many of the miracles in this book are, frankly, remarkable—which is part of what makes them miracles. Every effort was made to confirm and verify the stories through medical records, historical research, and eyewitness accounts. I feel confident that the miracles in this collection are authentic. To authenticate miracles, however, is not my ultimate aim. Instead, the stories in this book are intended to serve as an unmistakable reflection of God's power and love. When you read about the miracles, I hope you will believe them. More than that, though, I hope you will believe in the God who still works miracles in our midst.

—JODIE BERNDT

PART ONE

Miracles Happen

When God Comes Down

Always be in a state of expectancy, and see that you leave room
for God to come in as He likes.

—OSWALD CHAMBERS

BELIEVE IN MIRACLES. I always have, for as long as I can remember.
And according to a national survey taken in 1995, I am in
surprisingly strong company: Some 80 percent of all Americans say
they believe in the miraculous.[1]

Many of these folks, I imagine, have read about miracles, heard about them
from friends, or simply accepted their existence based on a general and
collective willingness to embrace the supernatural.

For me, though, the experience that tested my convictions was on a more
personal, intimate level.

Twelve years ago my younger sister, Jennifer, was diagnosed with colon cancer.
I was in college at the time and physically removed from the day-to-day
challenges she faced. Whether through genuine faith and optimism or a
protective desire to screen me from the actual danger Jen faced, my parents'
telephone calls to me were filled with reassuring—even upbeat—reports about
her condition.

For my part, ignorance really was bliss. I knew little—if anything—about cancer, and while I was sorry Jennifer was sick, I assumed her doctors would do some poking around, locate the problem, and have her back on her feet in no time at all. We had, in my family, routinely prayed for relief from such ailments as childhood fevers, sore throats, and skinned knees. Now, I thought, we were simply praying for something a little more important.

Looking back, I am amazed at my casual attitude. I remember laughing with Jennifer about all the weight she had lost. She had never been heavy, but as she battled the cancer she got down to about ninety pounds, and we both admired her *Glamour*-model chicken legs. It never occurred to me that Jennifer could have—and, according to at least one medical study *should have*—died.

It was only years later, when I began to hear about and meet other cancer patients, that I felt the full impact of my sister's illness—and, more significantly, of her miracle. How had she felt? Had she been afraid? Had she expected God to heal her? If so, why? If not, why not?

Over time, my curiosity grew, and I plied Jennifer with questions. I took notes on her answers. Some of them astounded me—both by what they revealed about the serious nature of her condition and by what they showed of her spirit. As I read my handwritten notes over and over again, Jennifer's story began to take shape...

MY SISTER'S MIRACLE

In the months before Jennifer's cancer was diagnosed, her doctors had prescribed iron pills to combat her increasing fatigue and anemia. Jen had also experienced intermittent bleeding over the years—but she never told anyone. By the time she was seventeen she felt confident that whatever it was would eventually go away. After all, she was a high school senior, spring was in the air, and there were more important things—like parties and proms—to worry about.

Then one day in May 1983, Jen and my mother were lying in our back yard, talking and laughing together in the warm spring sunshine. They had been having such fun—until the bulge appeared.

"Look, Mom," Jen said, pointing to her stomach. "Do you see that lump?"

Mom sat up and stared at Jennifer's stomach. Her concern mounted as the lump grew. Finally, there was a loud rumble and the protrusion was gone.

"See?" Jennifer asked. "It sounds like thunder Remember I told you about the time I was sitting in class? My stomach made such a loud noise the teacher stopped talking—and a man who was out in the hall opened the classroom door to find out what had happened!"

At the time, my sister had simply shrugged her shoulders and apologized to her classmates. "Sorry," she had said. "I'm having digestive trouble." The noises never bothered her much. For the past five years she had suffered painful bouts with what she thought was a mysterious digestive bug. As a result, she had missed a lot of school—and, she thought ruefully, she hadn't been a very fun date at the senior prom.

To Jennifer, the bulge was more of a curiosity than anything, but Mom saw things in a different light. That warm day in May, when she saw the lump grow in Jennifer's stomach, she got to her feet immediately and wrapped a towel around her swimsuit. "Come on," she said to Jennifer. "I'm taking you to the doctor."

Several days later the doctor delivered the stunning news: Jennifer had cancer. There was a malignant tumor growing in her colon—almost unheard of in someone her age. Surgery would be scheduled immediately.

"Surgery?" Jen looked first at Mom and Dad and then at the doctor. "I won't need surgery. God will heal me."

Jennifer stayed in the hospital, and tried to keep up the faith. Dad led her in searching the Bible for God's promises about healing and protection, and she taped them to her hospital-room wall, one above the other, so the doctors and nurses and every visitor who entered the room could not help but comment on the unusual wallpaper.

Still, the days went by, and Jennifer's condition remained unchanged. Surgery loomed ever closer. *Why*, Jen wondered, *is God taking so long with my miracle?*

Three days before her surgery Jennifer got her first miracle. Sitting on her hospital bed, she held our folks' hands as the three of them prayed. Suddenly, the words from a verse familiar to her consumed her mind: "Now to him who is able to do immeasurably more than all we ask or imagine, according to his power that is at work within us, to him be glory in the church and in Christ Jesus throughout all generations."[2]

Jennifer knew God had spoken to her. First, He was promising to do more than she was asking Him to do. Moreover, He would use Jennifer's situation to glorify Himself. In that instant, Jennifer realized exactly how she should pray. "Lord, do more than I am imagining or asking," she said, "and use this for Your glory!"

Suddenly Jennifer felt a peace unlike anything she had ever experienced. No longer would she put God in a box; everything was going to be okay—even if it meant she had to have an operation.

Word of Jen's condition spread. The local newspaper picked up her story and ran an article, complete with photographs of Jennifer and her patchwork wallpaper. Four follow-up pieces later, Jen found herself deluged with visitors, calls, and letters—many from people she had never met.

One card in particular caught Jen's attention. It was from a woman who, reeling from desperate financial circumstances, had decided to kill herself. Contemplating her choice, she had poured herself a cup of coffee and stared, distractedly, at the morning paper. There was Jennifer's picture, along with a mention of Jesus' healing.

The woman read the article. As the words sank into her mind, her outlook began to change. "If this teenager can find joy in the Lord," she resolved, "then so can I."

Another miracle.

On May 13, 1983, four days after her eighteenth birthday, Jennifer had surgery to remove the tumor. It had grown to the size of a grapefruit and was nestled against an artery. Positioned as it was next to some lymph nodes, the cancer had had every opportunity to spread throughout her bloodstream—particularly since it had festered, undetected, for so many years. To the doctors' amazement, though, they could find no traces of the cancer anywhere else in my sister's body. The nature of cancer is to grow, but as they put it, "Somehow, this tumor contained itself." Jennifer's third miracle.

Jennifer was ready to go home—but the medical team was not prepared to let her go just yet. Even though they couldn't find it, the doctors reasoned that Jen's body must contain some cancer traces because she had had the disease so long; as a result they recommended radiotherapy and chemotherapy treatments. The problem, however, was that radiation would destroy Jen's ability to have children.

Mom and Dad were not willing to accept the doctors' grim prognosis. Instead, they consulted a specialist at Georgetown/Medical Center University—a man reputed to be the top expert in cases such as Jennifer's. After a battery of tests and a thorough physical examination, the specialist pronounced Jennifer completely healthy.

With this fourth miracle, freedom was in sight. The only problem, as Jen saw it, was the colostomy she had undergone. She still wore a bag on her stomach to aid in digestion—and the doctors had warned that it would be two or three months before her colon was ready to work on its own. *Two or three months.* Our house was only a mile from the ocean, and summertime was just around the corner. Jen hated the thought of missing out on all the fun her friends would have at the beach.

She need not have worried. Two and a half weeks after her cancer surgery, she went back to the doctor. He examined her, dumbfounded. "I certainly can't explain it," he admitted, "but your colon is completely ready to go!"

But Jennifer's miracle was not over yet. Some time after her surgery she began to suspect a scar-tissue blockage, normal after an operation such as she had had. Jen returned to the doctor for additional tests. Not only was there no scar tissue, but the medical team could not find any evidence in her colon that she had ever had surgery! The "blockage" she felt was no more than a simple case of constipation.

Reflecting on God's goodness, Jennifer made a startling observation: "Even with the physical pain, this has been one of the best times in my life."

Perhaps nothing revealed the magnitude of my sister's miracle so clearly as a letter Jen received more than ten years later from the chief surgeon at the hospital where she had had her operation. After examining her the doctor wrote that Jen was "obviously free and clear of any risk of recurrence."

Noting that many cancer patients who had undergone radiotherapy and chemotherapy had, ten years down the road, developed second malignancies, the surgeon reflected on the importance of the decision Jennifer and our parents had made not to pursue this treatment. Moreover, he included a copy of an abstract of a report from a medical journal citing the rarity of colon cancer in children. Reporting on a twenty-eight-year study conducted on patients between the ages of ten and seventeen, the article noted that the aggressive nature of the cancer, coupled with atypical or confusing symptoms, led to a high mortality rate. Death occurred at an average of eleven months after diagnosis. Of the children studied during the twenty-eight years, there were no survivors.[3]

No survivors. "When one looks at the results suffered by other patients," the chief surgeon wrote, "one can only marvel at the miracle that Jennifer represents."

I have been marveling over Jennifer's miracle for the past twelve years. It seemed she had received so *many* miracles. I wanted to get all the details straight on things like the clean lymph nodes, the vanished scars, and all of the people—roommates, doctors, nurses, friends, and even strangers—who were touched by Jennifer's story. Which miracle, I wondered, was the greatest? Which one clinched Jen's awareness of God's intervention in her life?

I thought Jennifer might need some time to consider her answers, so I was surprised when she replied without hesitation. "What God did in each of those specific situations was great," she said. "But none of that is the real miracle. The real miracle is in how God used my experience for His glory. When I got home from the hospital I wrote down all the ways He was glorified—and I counted more than sixty-five different items."

MIRACLES DEFINED

Jennifer's story did not *generate* so much as it *cemented* my belief in miracles. Yet my proximity to her experience raised a whole new spectrum of questions. How, for example, could I explain to my more skeptical friends what had happened to Jen? How can you separate the miraculous from the merely fortunate, or the coincidental? How do you know what is truly miraculous?

For starters, I wanted a good definition of *miracle*. You hear the term everywhere these days: sports fans ogle replays of the "miracle" catch, cosmetic counters stock expensive vials of "miracle" cream, and unprepared students hope for a "miracle" come examination time. You can even buy "miracle" mayonnaise.

Yet even with such familiarity, the word retains an authoritative presence. The dictionary defines *miracle* as an "event or effect in the physical world beyond or out of the ordinary course of things, deviating from the known laws of nature."[4] C. S. Lewis said a miracle is an "interference with Nature by a supernatural power."[5] My favorite explanation, however, comes from Herbert Lockyer in his exhaustive study on the miracles of the Bible: "A miracle has been defined as a work wrought by a divine power for a divine purpose by means beyond the reach of man."[6]

In other words, God reaching down to touch our lives in a way we never could have done or even imagined. Do you believe God would reach down on your behalf today? Do you believe in miracles? My sister Jennifer did—yet she would have missed the best part of her miracle if she had not opened her eyes to God's bigger picture. As Oswald Chambers put it in his classic book, *My Utmost for His Highest,* "Do not look for God to come in any particular way, but look for Him."[7]

MIRACLES, MAGIC, AND MEN FROM MARS

Assuming the statistics are true and eight in ten Americans really do believe in miracles, I could envision Jennifer's story giving me a conversational "in" with the cocktail and dinner-party crowd. "Oh yes," I might say, "I believe in miracles. My sister was healed of cancer, you know."

But somehow, explaining Jennifer's miracle has not been that easy. People may say they believe in miracles, but, as popular Catholic author Dr. Ralph McInerny put it, "the Christian is well advised to realize that his own beliefs, including the belief that miracles occur, strike some nonbelievers as of apiece with stories of the Siberian who lived over two hundred years, of flying saucers, or reports of psychic phenomena."[8]

To differentiate Jen's story from those men-from-Mars type of accounts, I had always focused on the nuts and bolts of her story: the clean lymph nodes, the lack of scar tissue, the chief surgeon's letter—in short, the irrefutable "facts" of her experience. However, Jen's comment about what constituted the *real* miracle made me change my thinking. How *do* you know when a real miracle happens? How can you tell if you've been targeted by God?

One way is to look for the meaning behind the miracle. As two modern apologists put it, "God doesn't intervene just to play around and confuse us; He has a purpose and communicates something with each miracle."[9] In Jen's case, God's purpose was to glorify himself. This purpose fits well with McInerny's characterization of the miraculous. True miracles, he notes, are "not meant to amuse or divert or to frighten or titillate." Instead, they are always a "sign of God's presence and an opportunity for men to respond to the divine call."[10]

My hunch is that many of today's professed miracle believers have little knowledge of the true nature of God; instead, their "miracles" are more of the New Age, pantheistic, "may the Force be with you" variety. Such happenings cannot, therefore, present an opportunity for men to respond to God— meaning, in terms of their lasting or comprehensive impact, they are really no better than magic tricks.

Two thousand years ago in Samaria a man named Simon went around amazing everyone with his elaborate magic show. He was a sorcerer, and because of the feats he performed and his own boasting, people called him "the divine power" and followed him everywhere.

But one day Simon met his match—more than his match, in fact. Simon heard Philip preach about Jesus, and he became a believer. What caught Simon's attention even more than the good news about Jesus, however, were the signs and miracles Philip performed.

Simon watched Philip closely, trying in vain to spot the tricks. Finally, his curiosity got the better of him. He wanted desperately to do the same incredible things the apostles did, and he offered them money if they would only share their secrets. The apostle Peter—never one to sugarcoat his words—turned on Simon and replied, "[May] your money perish with you, because you thought that the gift of God could be purchased with money!"[11]

Peter knew what Simon did not: The power he and the other apostles demonstrated did not belong to them. Their miracles, like others recorded in the Bible, inspired awe, reflected God's power, and confirmed God's message and His messenger.[12] Because of these purposes, miracle power could never be attributed to anyone or anything other than God.

Lockyer pointed out that miracle workers had to disclaim any inherent power of their own. Moreover, they had to believe that God could indeed perform what was impossible from the human standpoint.[13] Few stories illustrate the distinction between genuine miracles and magic as well as that of Moses and the Egyptian magicians.

When Moses stood before Pharaoh to ask the Egyptian king to release the Israelites, Pharaoh demanded a miracle. Aaron immediately threw down the staff he was carrying, and it became a snake. Unwilling to admit that this miracle was from God, Pharaoh summoned his magicians. They took their staffs and repeated the miracle—only Aaron's snake devoured theirs.

Next, Moses turned the Nile into a river of blood and then called forth a plague of frogs—both at God's command. Again, Pharaoh's sorcerers copied the trick (although I have always felt a better feat would have been to get rid of the blood and the frogs). Finally, Moses turned all of the dust in Egypt into gnats. This time the magicians could not repeat the miracle. They turned to Pharaoh in defeat. "This," they said, "is the finger of God."[14]

POWER WITH A PURPOSE

R. C. Trench, a nineteenth-century scholar who wrote the widely respected and influential *Notes on the Miracles of Our Lord*, classified the miracles performed by the Egyptian magicians as more than mere conjurers' tricks. He maintained that their magic was rooted in "the spiritual powers of wickedness"—powers that were in direct conflict with the God of Israel. The key distinction between the two was that, while the magicians' feats paralleled those performed by Moses, they fell short of the truly miraculous because they had no relation to God's ultimate ends of grace, wisdom, and love.[15] In other words, the magicians' tricks demonstrated power but not purpose.

This, then, is the mark against which I hope the miracles in this book will be measured. As C. S. Lewis put it, the fitness of Christian miracles "lies in the fact that they show an invasion by a power that is not alien."[16] God knows us, and His miracles demonstrate His involvement in our lives. For a modern world that often embraces the supernatural without stopping to consider the *source* of the power, the stories recorded here will point to God's higher purpose—to His grace, His wisdom, and His love for each one of us.

A Case for Modern Miracles

If you begin by ruling out the supernatural you will perceive no miracles.

—C. S. LEWIS

A FRIEND OF MINE LIKES TO TELL THE STORY of what happened in a philosophy class at a Virginia university some years ago.

Every year the philosophy professor began the first day of his class with the same forceful questions. "Who here believes in God? Is God all powerful? Can He do miracles? Does He want to be known?"

Scanning his audience of eager minds, the professor held up a glass jar. "I'm holding this jar," he said. "Is there anyone here who will pray to God so that the jar will not break when I drop it?"

The challenge hung in the air. "Every year, for seventeen years, we've tried this experiment—and the jar always breaks. It breaks because God is not real or operative in today's world. Now, is there anyone here who wants to pray?"

Just as the professor had suspected, the room was silent. Suddenly, though, one boy spoke up. His tone was quiet but firm. "I'll pray that prayer," he said.

The professor was taken aback. No one, it seemed, had ever accepted his challenge. "Okay," he said. "What should we do? Should we bow our heads?"

"You can do whatever you like," the boy said simply. And then he prayed.

"God, I pray You would honor Your name today. Amen."

The anticipation was palpable as the professor lifted the jar. He released his hold—and the jar fell to the ground, struck the teacher's foot, and rolled to one side, intact.

The room erupted as students stood and stretched to see what had happened. There were some in the front row who swore they saw the jar's path curve inward as it fell. Others, however, put the matter down to a poorly executed drop by the eager professor.

WHY PEOPLE DON'T BELIEVE

Like the skeptical philosophy students, there will always be those who discount or explain away the miraculous. Jack Deere taught for ten years at Dallas Theological Seminary, where he maintained that God no longer performed miracles. There was no need for them, Deere reasoned, once people had the completed Bible to showcase God's presence and power. No person of any intelligence whatsoever could possibly believe otherwise.

To prove his point, Deere began an exhaustive study of the Bible—and, almost in spite of himself, came away "absolutely convinced that the Scriptures do not teach that the gifts of the Spirit passed away with the death of the apostles." Instead, Deere concluded, contemporary thinkers based their skepticism on the fallible wisdom of personal experience.

"There is one basic reason why Bible-believing Christians do not believe in the miraculous gifts of the Spirit today," Deere wrote. "It is simply this: *they have not seen them.*"[2]

A VISIT TO LOURDES

Malcolm Muggeridge, who confessed to a general distrust of miracles, might have fit Deere's profile of a skeptic. "I am by temperament an extremely sceptical person," he wrote. "I don't believe in a lot that people say about their religious experiences. I'm very sceptical about the fantasies of mysticism altogether. I don't believe in visions myself, since I have never had one."[3]

And yet even Muggeridge found himself caught up in the supernatural drama when he accompanied a band of pilgrims to the French city of Lourdes. Sick people have come to Lourdes since 1858, when a young French girl—acting in obedience to visions she had of the Virgin Mary—scratched the earth to release a miraculous spring that produced healing water. At first a mere trickle, the spring formed a pool within two days. Today millions of visitors flock to Lourdes each year to bathe in and even drink the miraculous water, which has been associated with thousands of supernatural cures.

On location in Lourdes merely to record the visit to the shrine for television viewers, Muggeridge had no high expectations for the journey. Yet the pilgrims' enthusiasm was contagious. Most of the group were sick or crippled, and many were on the verge of death. Muggeridge marveled at their fortitude, faith, and joy. In his crusty skepticism, however, he found little to say—until he noticed the exquisitely beautiful, luminous eyes of one dying girl. "What marvelous eyes!" he exclaimed.

Muggeridge found himself captivated by the emotion of the moment. It was, he wrote, "as though I saw God's love shining down on us visibly, in an actual radiance. That was my miracle at Lourdes."[4]

Muggeridge had become part of the Lourdes experience—where, as one scholar put it, "the most aggressive of egoists feels himself at one with the cripples, the paralytics, the epileptics, and the blind: even an unbeliever feels tempted to pray."[5] And even unbelievers must ultimately acknowledge the miraculous cures that take place at Lourdes. Since 1884, the *Bureau Medical* of Lourdes has enforced a stringent litmus test for substantiating miracles. To be accepted as a genuine miracle, a healing must manifest at least one of these five signs:

1. Absence of a curative agent.

2. Instantaneousness of the cure.

3. Suppression of convalescence.

4. Abnormality in the method of cure.

5. Recovery of the use of a function without the action of the appropriate organ that remains incapable of performing it.[6]

In addition to meeting these criteria, the miracles are analyzed by an international team of medical specialists. Each year between eight and fifteen hundred physicians participate in the examination process. Among the doctors who visited Lourdes in 1903 was Alexis Carrel, a Nobel-prize-winning physicist and a nonbeliever.

Considering it absurd to talk about miracles, Dr. Carrel vowed that he would not be influenced by anything he saw at Lourdes. One sick woman, however, caught his attention. Afflicted with tuberculosis at an early age, the lady suffered from an abdominal tumor that made her body hardly recognizable as human. Her doctors had given up on her.

As the nuns at Lourdes bathed the woman's stomach with water from the spring, Carrel watched her like a hawk. Even as one of his medical colleagues noted that the woman was dying, Carrel suddenly saw her features begin to change. Fixing his attention on the woman, Carrel watched as her condition rapidly and visibly improved until the blanket that covered her abdomen moved and the tumor, it seemed, disappeared.

Carrel could no longer restrain himself. "How do you feel?" he asked the woman.

"Very well," she replied. "I'm not strong, but I feel that I am cured."

Carrel examined the woman and confirmed her suspicions. The tumor was gone. She had, indeed, experienced a miracle. Casting aside his intellectual pride, Carrel—like so many skeptics before him—became a believer.[7]

A YEARNING TO BELIEVE

Not all skeptics exhibit the same reluctance to believe in miracles as Dr. Carrel. Jamie Buckingham, for example, had never witnessed a miracle. Like Deere, he had seen them neatly explained away at the hands of his seminary professors, who taught that miracles were over and that modern Christians were to accept God by faith, not sight. Moreover, Buckingham's professors shredded biblical miracles with their logic: Jesus did not walk on water; He was actually standing in a little boat the disciples could not see. He did not heal a blind man; rather, the Lord's touch released an "inner power" that broke through the man's self-induced blindness. And instead of literally calming the storm on the Sea of Galilee, Jesus gave His disciples a "miraculous" inner peace as the wind, coincidentally, died down of its own accord.[8]

Buckingham heard all these arguments, yet he secretly yearned to believe. But how could he? He had never seen a miracle, and frankly, the miracles Jesus performed seemed more like wonderful fairy tales than historical facts—until one happened to him. I love the way Buckingham tells his story:

MY WIFE ASKED ME to fix a leaky kitchen faucet. I am not much of a mechanic, a fact to which my sparse tools bore evidence. In the kitchen drawer I found an old screwdriver—one the children had pushed into a light socket some months before. The tip of the screwdriver was jagged with weld burns. After removing the faucet with a wrench, I went to work with that horrible screwdriver, trying to remove the corroded screw which held the rubber washer in place. Holding the fixture in my left hand and the screwdriver in my right, I pressed hard against the head of the brass screw. Suddenly the tip of the screwdriver slipped out of the screwhead and rammed, full force, into the soft place between my thumb and forefinger on my left hand. I dropped the fixture and howled with pain. Then, in a foolish reflex action, I yanked the screwdriver out of my hand. When I did a sizable chunk of flesh came out with it—clinging to the jagged edges of the welded tool.

Blood spurted everywhere and I shouted for my wife. Running into the kitchen, she saw all the blood and began screaming. I slid to the floor, holding my right hand over the spurting wound, as I gasped for her to "get me something." I assumed she knew I was talking about a washcloth or compress. Instead, she ran out the front door, apparently heading to the neighbor's house to ask for prayer.

Sitting in a growing puddle of blood, I began to feel weak.

"What would Jesus do if He were here?" I asked myself.

I knew what He would do. He would reach out, touch my wounded hand, and it would be healed.

Then I thought. If Christ is really, really in me—why don't I let Him do it through me? Still holding my right hand over the deep, open wound, I began to pray.

As Buckingham prayed, he lost track of time. His pain subsided, and he noted, vaguely, that the bleeding had stopped. Yet what captured his attention more than the wound was the "wonder of the prayer," the sense of communing and fellowshipping with God. When he finally opened his eyes, there stood his wife, looking down at him. He thought she had been gone for an hour, but only three or four minutes had passed. Here is where Buckingham's story gets really interesting:

GINGERLY, I REMOVED MY RIGHT HAND from the wound. The spot between my thumb and forefinger where the ragged screwdriver had penetrated was still covered with blood. My wife knelt beside me and handed me a damp cloth. As I wiped away the blood I was aware the wound had closed. Not only had it closed, it had healed over. There was no gaping hole, no cut, not even an indentation. All I could see was a tiny scar, like a wrinkle in my hand. My wife examined my hand also. It was healed.

That night, when I went to bed, I kept rubbing my finger over the place where the ugly wound had been. There was no roughness, no soreness. I knew, drifting off to sleep, as I know today, that the day of miracles has not passed. Jesus is not only alive. He is alive in me.[9]

WOULD GOD DO THAT?

Doubt concerning the miraculous—and even scoffing or cynicism—is a staple of modern thought. Most of us have never experienced the divine touch Buckingham felt. We will probably never approach the subject of miracles with the determination and scrutiny exhibited by Deere as he raked and sifted the Scriptures. Instead, we will be surrounded by a popular theology that discounts the miraculous even as it dismisses the power of God.

C. S. Lewis captured the contemporary mind-set, noting that people are willing to embrace beauty, truth, and goodness, or even a "spiritual force." They do not, however, cotton to a God who has "purposes and performs particular actions, who does one thing and not another, a concrete, choosing, commanding, prohibiting God with a determinate character." Popular religious thinkers exclude miracles, according to Lewis, because they exclude the "living God" of Christianity and choose, instead, a "kind of God who obviously would not do miracles, or indeed anything else."[10]

THE DOUBTING-THOMAS SYNDROME

Does such a skeptical, or reluctant, attitude offend the Lord? Jesus was certainly no stranger to scoffing; time and again—as when He approached the house of Jairus to heal the man's lifeless daughter—Christ encountered mockery and laughter.[11] Yet consider His response to one of history's most famous skeptics, "doubting" Thomas, who was not present when the Lord first appeared to the other disciples after His resurrection.

Can you picture Thomas returning from the market or some other errand and finding the other disciples who had just been with Jesus? They were, I imagine, delirious with delight over the fact that their Lord was alive.

"Hey," Thomas asked. "What's going on?"

"It's Jesus! He's alive! We've seen Him!" James and John were talking so fast their words formed an excited jumble.

"Whoa—hold on fellas." Thomas eyed his friends warily. If this was their idea of a good joke—well, it was not very funny. Thomas knew where Jesus had been buried. He wasn't buying their crazy story.

"I'll tell you what," he challenged. "I saw what happened to Jesus. I know how He died. And unless I see the nail marks—no, unless I touch His hands, well, I simply can't believe He is alive. And, for that matter, I want to put my hand into His side. He had a big hole there, remember?"

Thomas's skepticism did little to dampen the other disciples' enthusiasm. As they continued their revelry, he felt like an outsider. Never, in fact, had he felt so alone. If only what they said were true. If only Jesus really were alive.

A week later, the group met together again. This time Thomas was with them. The doors were locked—Thomas had made sure of that. The disciples weren't exactly popular with some of the big brass in town, and Thomas didn't want any trouble.

Suddenly, despite the locked doors, someone else was there.

Could it be? Was it possible? Thomas refused to believe his eyes. There stood Jesus—and He was looking straight at Thomas!

"See My hands?" Jesus said. "Put your finger here." It was a command, yet the Lord's voice was gentle. "Reach out your hand and put it into My side."

Thomas felt the hairs on the back of his neck stand up. Who was this man?

The Lord had not taken His eyes off Thomas. "Stop doubting," He said, "and believe."

Thomas had heard enough. Here was his Lord, alive—and in the flesh! "My Lord and my God!" It wasn't an eloquent confession, but it was enough. Thomas had become a believer.[12]

Jesus understands the human heart. Instead of rebuking Thomas for his skepticism, the Lord met his demand for proof. I suspect He knew that Thomas—like Buckingham—yearned to believe in miracles.

FACTS...OR FAIRY TALES?

In assigning a purpose to the miraculous, medieval writers recognized a distinction between belief and skepticism: "Unbelievers are excited to believe by miracles, and they also confirm faith, so that wonders animate the faithful and confound believers."[13] In other words, as two contemporary authors have put it, miracles are, to the believer, "a wonderful confirmation of the power and message of God, but to the unbeliever, miracles are a stumbling block—a proof that religion is just a bunch of fairy tales after all."[14]

Miracles may represent a stumbling block for the skeptic—but the block is never big enough to thwart the hand of God. Remember Naaman, the leper? He had heard that Elisha could cure his leprosy—but when the prophet told him what to do, Naaman balked. Reading the biblical account of this story, I can imagine the scene.

Naaman, the valiant army commander, arrived at Elisha's house with an entourage of his finest chariots. Perhaps Elisha heard Naaman's horses as they stomped and pawed the ground outside his humble door—yet he ignored the military fanfare. Instead of rushing out to greet the famous commander, the prophet sent a simple assistant to deliver a message. "Go wash yourself seven times in the Jordan," the man told Naaman, "and your flesh will be restored."

How Naaman's jaw must have dropped! The Jordan was nothing—merely a dirty stream in comparison to the vast rivers he knew at home. Wash seven times? Naaman did not like to expose his leprosy to anyone—and he was not about to make a spectacle of himself with repeated dips into some foul foreign river. And furthermore, who did Elisha think he was, sending out a mere servant boy! Naaman had expected some sort of ceremony—a full-blown healing service with hands waving and Elisha up there, praying away to his God. Was this some sort of a practical joke? Unable to control himself, Naaman stormed off in a rage.

Fortunately for Naaman, his servants had the guts to go after him. With their persuasion, he finally made his way down to the Jordan. Envision the setting as the great soldier slipped into the water:

One dip. *Nothing.* Two dips. Still no change. Three dips This is ridiculous. Four dips. *Maybe I should climb out now and salvage what little dignity I have left.* Five dips. *How will I face my army after this fiasco?* Six dips. *Just wait 'til I get my hands on that crazy prophet.* Seven dips. *Clean. Clean! Oh my goodness! It worked!* "Elisha! Where are you? I'm clean! It worked! Hallelujah—the Lord is God!"[15]

Chances are, Naaman had never seen a miracle. He only heard about Elisha through his wife's Israelite servant girl. Yet in his heart of hearts, underneath his skeptical bravado, Naaman desperately wanted to be healed. He had the heart of a seeker.

In one sense, Naaman reminds me of a Texan named Billy Moore. Like Naaman, Billy had never experienced the supernatural. He did not understand how healing worked—but, like Naaman, Billy was desperate for a miracle.

YESTERDAY, TODAY, AND FOREVER
Billy Moore did not feel well at all. His headaches had grown so severe that he

no longer was able to operate the heavy cranes on the construction site where he worked, Billy finally went to his doctor.

"I need a flu shot," Billy said.

The doctor stared at Billy. "Bill," he said slowly, "you don't have the flu. You have a malignancy."

"A what?"

"A malignancy."

The doctor had not yet examined Billy or done any tests. "How can you tell I have a malignancy?" Billy demanded.

"Well, I can tell something's wrong just by looking at you," the doctor replied, hoisting his medical journal from the shelf. "Your right pupil is the size of a pin, your eyelid is drooping, and you are only sweating on one side of your forehead. Look," he pointed to a page in his book, "you have the symptoms of a very rare malignancy."

Billy did not know what to think. He sat, stunned, as a second doctor agreed with the diagnosis and referred him to a specialist at a nearby hospital. A series of x rays confirmed the physician's fears: Billy had a tumor lodged in a nerve duct behind his eye.

Billy wondered how much work he would have to miss.

His doctor, however, had far more serious concerns. "This is a very delicate operation," the physician advised. "The tumor has grown into your nerve. In order to get to it, we'll have to go in through your skull." Billy heard the doctor as through a fog, yet the message was clear: The surgery could only guarantee a 50 percent success rate—but to forego it was to invite certain death as the cancer grew.

Billy wondered how his wife, Ruby, would take the news. He knew she would be upset and probably scared. Strangely, though, Billy wasn't frightened. He had been reading about the miracles that Jesus and His disciples did in the Bible, and—despite his church's denial of modern miracles—he could not escape the eternal promise: "Jesus Christ is the same yesterday, today, and forever."[16] Billy believed that the same God who went around healing folks almost two thousand years ago could—and would—heal him.

That afternoon, after Billy told his wife all about the malignancy, he took her hands in his own. "Ruby," he said, "God's going to remove my tumor."

"Billy!" Ruby cried, exasperated with her husband's simple faith, "God doesn't do things like that!"

"Why not?"

"Because we've been taught that He doesn't—that's why not!"

Ruby's words rang true. Never had they heard that God was still in the miracle business; in fact, many in their church doubted that He had ever done all those amazing things in the Bible—at least not in the literal sense.

Ruby was still talking. "Honey," she said, "you're going to have to trust the doctors on this one." She had enough to worry about with Billy's illness; the last thing she needed was for him to start filling her head with his crazy talk about healing.

A few nights later Billy couldn't sleep. So convinced had he been of God's ability to heal, he had refused the codeine pills his doctors prescribed. Now the pain was becoming unbearable. He checked his watch: 2:00 A.M.

Billy staggered to the medicine cabinet and emptied four pills into his hand. Before he could open his mouth, he was interrupted by a quiet voice, speaking somewhere inside his head. *Who are you going to trust?* the voice asked, *Me, or the medicine?*

Immediately Billy replaced the pills and made his way back to bed. He knew he had heard from the Lord—and, within moments, his pain was gone and he fell fast asleep.

When he awoke the next morning, Ruby was already up. Billy rolled over and looked at the clock radio. It was seven o'clock, and a local church's radio program was just starting.

"Good morning!" the announcer's voice boomed. "We're having a prayer meeting today. If you're sick, we'll pray for you—and God will heal you."

Get up and go.

Billy ignored the voice, thinking it had come from the radio. He was just slipping back into dreamland when the voice came again, audibly this time: "Get up and go!"

Billy sat up, startled. His eyes searched the room. No one was there.

He lost no time getting dressed. Stuffing his feet into his shoes, he hurried to find his car keys in the kitchen.

"What are you doing?" Ruby asked. "Where on earth are you going?"

"To a prayer meeting," Billy said, hastily smoothing his rumpled hair.

"But our church doesn't have prayer meetings!" Ruby protested.

"I've found one that does. And God told me to go."

Ruby turned away in contempt. First God was going to heal him, and now Billy was hearing voices. How long would she have to put up with this nonsense?

When Billy arrived at the church he found the doors locked. It was nine o'clock, and the place looked deserted. Had he come twenty-five miles for nothing?

"Okay, God," Billy challenged. "I'll give You one more chance. I'm going to drive around the block and come back. Remember—this whole thing was Your idea."

Slowly Billy cruised the side streets. He returned to the church parking lot, hardly daring to hope. But yes—someone was there! A man was unlocking the doors to the sanctuary.

"Hey! Excuse me!" Billy hurried to reach the man. "Are you the pastor?"

"Yes I am. Please, come inside."

Without a word Billy slipped into the church and sank into a pew. He was only alone for a moment before ten or eleven elderly women came in behind him.

"There were all these old grannies," Billy later reflected. "One had an accordion, one played the fiddle, and one sat down at the piano. Then they started singing and clapping—and I knew I wasn't in any church like I'd ever seen before!"

When the grannies finished singing, the pastor stood up to speak. He preached a brief sermon and then turned to Billy.

"We have a guest here this morning," the minister said. "Sir, please come up here so we can pray for you."

As Billy obliged, the grannies crowded around him. One woman reached into her bag for a bottle of oil.

Ugh, Billy thought, *castor oil.* How well he remembered the childhood battles with his own grandmother over the foul-tasting medicine. But if these sweet old ladies wanted him to drink their oil, well, he reckoned he could probably manage.

But the women surprised Billy. They did something he had never seen before. After wetting their fingers with a small drop of oil, they gently touched his head and began to pray. Even more surprising was what happened next: As the group prayed, Billy felt the pain disappear from his head. One moment it was there; the next, it was totally gone.

Billy couldn't wait to tell his wife the good news. He raced home and burst through the door. "Ruby!" he shouted. "I've got my healing!"

"You got your *what*?"

"My healing! In my head! The pain is gone!"

"You did not." Ruby was adamant. "The doctors want to see you tomorrow morning at eight o'clock. They've scheduled you for some more tests. And they want to go ahead with the operation."

Not even Ruby's skepticism could steal Billy's joy. In obedience to what he sensed was the Lord's direction, he agreed to go for the tests—if only, he maintained, to prove to Ruby and anyone else who asked—that he really was healed.

The next morning, as Billy tugged at his less-than-adequate hospital gown, he could not contain his enthusiasm. The headaches had not returned, and he was eager for the doctors' report.

Meanwhile, Ruby waited in the hospital lounge. As the hours dragged on, her fears grew. Surely they must have decided to operate, she reasoned. What else could be taking so long?

What was taking so long was a series of x rays and CAT scans that spanned eight hours. When Billy finally appeared, skipping down the hall in his hospital gown, Ruby could not believe her eyes.

"What did they do to you?" she asked, searching for some sign of a surgical incision.

"Nothing! They can't find anything. God healed me—just like I told you!"

Ruby felt her legs give way beneath her. She and Billy sat down, and in a few moments the doctor joined them.

"I do not have an explanation for this," he said. "The tumor is gone. It has disappeared."

Billy cut in. "I have an explanation, Doc. It's like you said: The tumor is gone."

"Yes, well, it certainly looks that way." The doctor extended his hand. "You do not have to come back, Mr. Moore."

As the doctor turned to leave, Ruby's eyes caught Billy's. "They *missed* it," she said. Billy just smiled. In time, he knew, she too would believe.

WHO CAN FATHOM THE MIND OF GOD?

In the course of researching and writing this book, I spoke with scores of people who knew of or had experienced the miraculous. Many of their stories are recorded here. Others, however, are still waiting for their miracles—and for some, doubt and skepticism have begun to creep into their thinking.

Kathryn Kuhlman was perhaps the most famous—and admittedly controversial—faith healer of her time. As an evangelist, she held services that attracted the world—from Hollywood stars to military generals to millions of "regular" folks who longed to see and believe in the miraculous. Her death in 1976 made front-page headlines across the country.

Many people received healings in Kuhlman's services—often in whole waves, as the Spirit "moved." Others, however, felt nothing. After traveling with her for some time, Kuhlman's biographer finally felt compelled to ask a point-blank question:

> "WHY ARE SOME NOT HEALED in your miracle services? How do you explain the fact that many leave, broken and disillusioned, while others are miraculously healed?"
>
> [Kuhlman] never hesitated. "The only honest answer I can give is: I do not know. Only God knows, and who can fathom the mind of God?"[17]

Who can predict when—and how—God will choose to reveal Himself through the supernatural? C. S. Lewis wrote of modern man's sudden shock upon discovering that his comfortable pantheistic God—one who demands and does nothing—is, in reality, God Himself, approaching and alive:

> THERE COMES A MOMENT when the children who have been playing at burglars hush suddenly: was that a *real* footstep in the hall? There comes a moment when people who have been dabbling in religion ("Man's search for God"!) suddenly draw back. Supposing we really found Him? We never meant it to come to *that!* Worse still, supposing He had found us?

So it is a sort of Rubicon. One goes across; or not. But if one does, there is no manner of security against miracles. One may be in for *anything*.[18]

The unpredictable nature of miracles is part of what makes them so fascinating. Whether you are a believer or a skeptic, the theology and practice of miracles provides for stimulating conversation and thought. Then, too, we are captivated by their dynamic power, by what miracles reveal about the "approaching and alive" character of God.

God's advance may be unmistakable, but there is nothing steamrollerish about it. His is not an indiscriminate, tornado-like force. Instead, as the coming chapter demonstrates, He comes alongside us, gracefully—yet mightily—catching us up in the miracle through the power of prayer.

Prayer Matters

We are not here to prove God answers prayer;
we are here to be living monuments of God's grace.

— OSWALD CHAMBERS

ALLY HOPKINS EASED HER GREEN BUICK LESABRE into the traffic flow. Up ahead, at the corner, she could see the red circle of the stoplight—no, now the signal was green. Sally smiled to herself. She must be living right.

Sally reached the intersection and began a left turn. Suddenly, she heard an audible voice. "Pray for your father," came the command. "He may die."

Almost as a reflex, Sally began to pray. She glanced quickly around the interior of her car and scanned the street outside. Where had the voice come from? It had sounded like someone was right there beside her—and yet, she reflected, the words had also come from outside, from all around the car. Brushing aside these thoughts, Sally concentrated on her father. She had to pray. And she needed to find a telephone.

Four rings. Five. Six. As her hands gripped the telephone receiver, Sally's heart began to pound. Where could her parents be? Dad, she realized, could be making rounds at the hospital where he served as chaplain when he wasn't working on his Sunday sermons, but Mom should be home. It was almost dinnertime.

Sally's calculations were not far off: Moments earlier, Mary and Tom Hopkins had been at home. Mary had busied herself with dinner preparations while Tom dozed in his favorite chair. It had been a long day at the hospital, and he was looking forward to a good night's rest.

Without warning, Tom began gasping for breath. Mary heard him and quickly fetched his inhaler. Another asthma attack. Tom had been sick so much recently; his asthma, it seemed, had begun to affect his entire system. Lately, the sudden attacks had become so common that Tom and Mary had almost come to expect them.

This time, though, something was different. The attack was not passing; instead, it appeared to be strengthening its hold on Tom.

"Tom." Mary tried to keep the panic out of her voice. "Tom, are you okay?" Even as she asked the question, Mary knew her husband could not respond. She hurried to the telephone to summon an ambulance. Every minute mattered.

When the emergency squad arrived, Mary watched, numb, as the medics administered oxygen and gave Tom some kind of a shot. She felt so helpless. The crew hoisted Tom into the waiting ambulance, and Mary caught sight of her husband's face. He was not responding.

One of the firefighters of the emergency squad drove Mary in her car to the hospital. In the waiting room she was glad for the familiar face of the family doctor she and Tom had known and trusted for years. When he spoke, however, her confidence evaporated.

"Mary," the doctor said gently, "you'd better call someone to come and stay with you. Try to get hold of your family; Tom looks pretty bad."

The doctor had seen Tom's charts. His lungs were overinflated, his pulse was almost nonexistent, and his skin was cold. The doctor dropped his voice. "I don't like having to tell you this, Mary, but we don't expect Tom to make it."

But Tom did make it. In fact, his recovery was so fast that, after five days in the intensive care unit, he was released from the hospital. Sunday morning found him back in his church pulpit, thankful his ordeal was over and marveling at God's goodness.

When Sally reflected on her father's brush with death and his surprising recovery, her mind kept returning to the voice in her car. God, she knew, had told her to pray. Had her obedience to His command played a role in saving her father's life? Did God really need her prayers?

Author Catherine Marshall would have understood Sally's questions. Marshall wondered why an omnipotent God, knowing our needs, could not supply them without waiting for our prayers. Why couldn't God simply give us what we need?

I love the picture of God's character that Marshall's explanation reveals: "He could, of course, but that is not His plan for His children on earth. Instead, He has dared arrange it so that He is actually dependent upon us in the sense of our prayers being necessary and all-important to the carrying out of His will on earth."[1]

God waits on our prayers. This arrangement may work in theory, yet there is an obvious flaw in the plan: Most of us do not know how to really pray; nor do we have any deep desire to do so. It is for this reason, Marshall noted, that we must depend on the Holy Spirit—the One who creates in us a basic desire to pray and who "spotlights for us the prayer-need or topic for prayer by creating a 'concern' within us."[2]

PROMPTED TO PRAY

This concern—or burden, as it is sometimes called—is what prompts people like Becky Beatenbo to spend anywhere from fifteen minutes to two hours at a time praying for men and women she hardly knows—or, in some cases, has never met.

In one instance, for example, Becky could not shake Rae McClellan's name from her mind. Becky had met Rae at church, and the two greeted one another as casual acquaintances if they happened to see one another on Sundays. One morning, as Becky prepared to run a few errands, she sensed the Spirit leading her to pray for Rae.

"Lord," Becky prayed, "send Your ministering angels to encamp about Rae and to guard her from all harm."

Rae stayed on Becky's mind all week long. By Saturday, her concern had grown so intense she could not do even the simplest task without first praying for Rae. Finally, Becky confided in her husband.

"Virgil," she said, "I'm not sure why, but God has kept Rae McClellan on my heart all week long. I've been praying for her every day."

Then, as suddenly as it had come, Becky's burden lifted. Becky sensed a release, and she wondered whether she would ever know why she had had such concern for Rae. She did not wonder long, however; the following morning, as Becky and Virgil sat in church, the minister made a stunning announcement.

"We thank God today for His protection. Some of you may know that yesterday morning Rae McClellan was in a very serious car accident. Her car struck a power pole at sixty miles per hour and, according to the police, Rae ought to be dead—but she's not. She's here today."

As the minister recounted Rae's experience, Becky gave Virgil a knowing look. Rae was sitting in the congregation less than twenty feet away, and as far as they could see, she did not have a scratch on her.

Later, they found out more about the accident. The impact of the collision had moved the power pole four feet across the ground and totally demolished Rae's Range Rover. The policeman who witnessed the scene said there was "no way she should have survived" the crash. Doctors concurred—after searching in vain for the damage they expected to find: a ruptured spleen, punctured lungs, broken ribs, or a spinal injury. Apart from a few cuts from the broken windshield, Rae was virtually untouched by the force of the collision.

Rae's experience may have amazed the police and her doctors, but the story made complete sense to Becky. As an intercessor, she is often unaware of the reasons or specific problems for which the Lord prompts her to pray. Months may pass before she discovers the purpose behind her prayers; sometimes she never knows. But such ignorance can be advantageous, according to Oswald Chambers. "If you know too much, more than God has engineered for you to know," he wrote, "you cannot pray, the condition of the people is so crushing."[3]

For the prayer novice, such uncertainty may create reluctance or hesitancy. Jack Deere noted that praying, particularly for something supernatural such as angelic protection or divine healing, typically involves some risk—specifically, "the risk of looking foolish."[4]

Deere's comment reminds me of an event that took place some twenty years ago. For several years during the 1970s my family spent two weeks of every summer in the Hamptons on Long Island. We attended a Christian family camp—one of several camps under the CFO umbrella. CFO stood for "Camp Farthest Out," and when I look back on some of the things that happened during those weeks, I guess the title fit.

Prayer groups of ten or fifteen people met regularly during the camp week. In my mother's group there happened to be an old Jewish man. He seemed a bit out of place at the camp—not so much because of his Jewishness as because of the shoes he wore. In an era when bare feet were more the rule than the exception, it seemed odd that this fellow always wore shoes. We never saw him take them off. Even at the beach, he wore a swimsuit and those shoes.

One day, during one of the scheduled prayer times, my mother felt the Lord telling her to pray for this old man's foot. Stranger still, she felt compelled to walk across the room and put her forehead down on his left shoe. "I didn't know what I was doing," she told me later. "I just sensed that God was at work, and I felt honored to be part of what was going on."

What was going on was incredible. Shortly after Mom finished praying, the group broke for lunch. The old man had not said a word. But as Mom rounded us up for the meal, we heard a commotion of sorts going on outside.

There, on the back porch, stood the old Jew. His shoes were off, and he was removing his left sock. When his companions saw his toe, they were amazed. It had been, they testified, completely black as the result of gangrene. Now the toe was perfectly normal. Better than normal, according to my mother. "It was fresh and pink and kissable," she said. "Just like a newborn baby's!"

As things turned out, the old fellow was a diabetic. The gangrene in his toe had become so advanced he was scheduled for surgery the following week to have the toe removed. I cannot help but wonder: If my mother had resisted the impulse to pray because she might look foolish (which, no doubt, she did), would that man have lost his toe? More importantly, would he—and everyone else who witnessed the miracle—have been denied the privilege of seeing God's hand at work?

I do not know. What I am convinced of, though, is that the words of James 5:16 are true: The prayer of a righteous man (or woman) is powerful and effective.

POWERFUL AND EFFECTIVE PRAYER

Certainly John Wesley would be counted as one of history's righteous men. His legacy spans the centuries, bolstered by his hymns, sermons, and contributions to Methodism. One writer, in fact, describes him as "the hero of an epic written and stage-managed by God himself."[5]

I have long admired Wesley for his tireless commitment to proclaiming the gospel and the steadfastness of his faith. What I failed to recognize, however, was what a controversial figure he was. I had always lumped him together with the Methodists I knew: likable people who raised good families, went to church on Sundays and for Wednesday suppers, and did not go poking about very often in the realm of the supernatural.

How different is the picture I formed after reading Wesley's journals! It was not at all uncommon to find folks falling over as though dead as Wesley preached while others groaned so loudly over sin and righteousness that they all but drowned him out.[6] As a result of these antics, many in the church leadership turned their backs on Wesley's ministry. On several occasions, in fact, the mere rumor of Wesley's presence was enough to inspire a lynch mob.

I love how Wesley responded in these situations—both for what it reveals about him, and more significantly, for what it shows regarding the power of prayer. Once, when he had gone to visit a sick woman, an angry crowd formed outside her home. "A louder or more confused noise, could hardly be at the taking of a city by storm," Wesley wrote.

"Bring out the Methodist! Bring out the Methodist!" The chant of the mob grew louder and louder. Fearing for their lives, Wesley's hosts fled, leaving him with a young servant girl. As the rabble forced their way into the home, the poor girl was terrified.

"O sir," she pleaded with Wesley, "what must we do?"

"We must pray," said Wesley.

"But, sir, is it not better for you to hide yourself? To get into the closet?"

"No," Wesley replied. "It is best for me to stand just where I am."

By this time some impatient sailors had joined the mob, and pushing the crowd out of the way, they tore the door to Wesley's room off its hinges. Immediately Wesley stepped forward. "Here I am," he said. "Which of you has anything to say to me? To which of you have I done any wrong? To you? Or you?"

Wesley continued walking and talking until he reached the street. Raising his voice, he addressed the mob.

"Neighbors, countrymen! Do you desire to hear me speak?"

"Yes! Yes!" came the vehement reply. "He shall speak. He shall. Nobody shall hinder him." *Here was the crowd bent on assaulting Wesley just moments earlier, miraculously quieted by the power of prayer!*

Wesley spoke, and as far as his voice carried, the people were still. Wesley thus preached his way through the town until, at last, he was rescued by a levelheaded clergyman and a couple of local politicians who ushered him into a house and then hustled him out the back door. As the abandoned mob regained its fury, Wesley slipped away in a small boat that carried him to his next destination.

Reflecting on his escape, Wesley marveled at the hand of God:

HERE, ALTHOUGH THE HANDS of perhaps some hundreds of people were lifted up to strike or throw, yet they were one and all stopped in the midway; so that not a man touched me with one of his fingers; neither was anything thrown from first to last; so that I had not even a speck of dirt on my clothes. Who can deny that God heareth the prayer, or that he hath all the power in heaven and earth?[7]

Wesley's understanding of the power of prayer has been echoed by believers throughout the centuries. One of the most dramatic illustrations of the vitality and importance of this kind of Spirit-led prayer came to me via a missionary's letter. It contained a report from a medical missionary who was home on furlough.

Here is the fellow's story as he shared it with his home church:

WHILE SERVING AT A SMALL FIELD HOSPITAL in Africa, I traveled by bicycle through the jungle to a nearby city every two weeks for supplies, a journey of two days requiring a camping overnight at the halfway point.

On one of those journeys I arrived in the city to collect money from a bank, purchase medicine and supplies, and begin my two-day journey back to the field hospital. Upon arrival in the city I observed two men fighting. One man had been seriously injured so I treated him for his injuries, while at the same time witnessing to him of the Lord Jesus. I then traveled back the two days, camping overnight, and arrived without incident.

Two weeks later I repeated my journey. Upon arriving in the city, I was approached by the young man I had treated two weeks earlier. He told me that he had known that I carried money and drugs (medicine). He said, "Some friends of mine and I followed you into the jungle, knowing that you would camp overnight. We were waiting just outside of your campsite for you to go to sleep. We were then going to kill you and take your money and drugs. But just as we were about to move into your campsite, we observed and counted 26 armed guards standing around you."

At this I laughed and said that I was certainly all alone out in that jungle campsite. The young man pressed the point and said, "No sir, I was not the only person to see the guards. My five friends also saw them, and we all counted them. It was because of those 26 guards that we were afraid and left you alone."

At this point in the church service, one of the men jumped to his feet and interrupted my story. He asked me, "Sir, can you tell me the exact day that this incident happened?" It took me a moment to recall, but I could. When I gave the date it happened, the man who had interrupted me told his story...

"When it is night in Africa, it is day here. On the night of your incident in Africa, it was morning here and I was preparing to go play a game of golf. As I was putting my golf bag in the car, I felt the Lord leading me to pray specifically for you. In fact, the urging was so strong that I called several of the men in this church together to meet with me here in the sanctuary and pray for you.

Would all of those men who met with me on that morning please stand up?"

The men who met together to pray that day stood. The number was exactly—26.[8]

I have read that story over and over again, and it never fails to amaze me. The twenty-six guards represent an astounding display of God's miraculous provision. Equally significant, though, is the miracle of the intercessor's obedience. How many of us, on our way to an appointment—from the golf course to the grocery store—would cast aside our own agenda in order to respond to and obey a sudden urge to pray?

Marshall attributes such promptings to the Holy Spirit, whom she calls "the Helper." Encouraging her readers to be sensitive to the Spirit's leading, she offers a prayer we are invited to borrow:

> FATHER, THIS IS THE PROMISE I make to You: when the Helper prompts me to pray, I will drop what I'm doing and pray; when I feel a concern for someone, I will talk with You about it and seek Your direction. Keep me alert to the Helper's tug at my sleeve, and give me, Lord, as a gift, a high level of willingness to obey and to follow through.[9]

HOW TO PRAY FOR MIRACLES

If the story of the twenty-six guards showcases God's modern-day might, Luke's account of Jairus's daughter offers a biblical glimpse into that same dramatic power. Jairus was a synagogue ruler—yet, when we meet him in Luke's narrative, he does not look very important or official. Instead, he has fallen at Christ's feet and is begging the Lord to come to his house. Jairus's twelve-year-old daughter—his only daughter—was dying.

Was Jairus a believer in miracles? Maybe so. Or maybe his perspective was newly acquired; as Deere observed, "Divine healing does not seem very important until we reach the point where physicians and modern medicine cannot help us."[10]

Regardless of Jairus's mind-set, he needed a miracle. Imagine his anguish, then, when the messenger arrived: "Your daughter is dead," he said. "Don't bother the teacher anymore."

How would we have responded in this instance? Would we have prayed for her recovery? Probably not. The image of my mother impulsively putting her forehead on an old man's shoe would pale in comparison to the seeming foolishness of praying for a dead person.

But Jesus has no such concern for appearances. Nor does He doubt the power of God. Instead, He turned to Jairus, and with words of reassurance, He encouraged the distraught father to "believe, and she will be made well."[11]

With that, Jesus made straight for Jairus's home, silenced the wailing mourners, and took the dead child by the hand. With only three of His friends and the little girl's parents watching Him, Jesus simply said, "Little girl, arise." At once, Luke tells us, the girl stood up—much to the astonishment of her parents.[12]

Jesus expected a miracle. There are, as Marshall pointed out, three vital elements in Christ's trust—the same three elements we need to adopt in order to pray effectively. First, *Christ believed power belongs to God.* Jesus did not stop to think about how foolish or insane He would appear if nothing happened when He prayed; instead, He concentrated on God's ability to give life to Jairus's daughter.

Next, *Christ recognized God's loving nature.* Throughout the Gospels, Jesus likens His Father to the most loving human father we can know or imagine. God loves us—and because of His great love, He wants to meet our needs.

Finally, *Jesus knew God had given Himself the freedom to stoop down and intervene in human affairs.* As Marshall put it, "He does reach down to answer our prayers. Were He, in fact, rigidly encased and bound by the natural laws of the universe

41

He Himself had called into being, then the miracles as recorded in the gospel narrations could never have happened."[13]

AWAITING ADVENTURE

This act of reaching down to touch our lives is the common theme in defining and understanding miracles. It is what gives us, like Jesus, the confidence to pray and expect an answer. And if God is willing to take an active part in our lives, then we must ask ourselves: Are we willing to let Him? Are we willing, as James charges, to pray for the sick and actually expect them to be healed?

If so, adventure awaits. Once we grasp the significance of prayer and the miracle-working power of God, we open ourselves up to the incredible.

One of the best word pictures of what could happen—indeed, what should happen—in churches today comes from author Annie Dillard in her book, *Teaching a Stone to Talk.*

Dillard suspects that when churchgoers routinely address the "Holy, Holy, Holy Lord, God of power and might," we have no idea what sort of power we so casually invoke. "It is madness," she wrote, "to wear ladies' straw hats and velvet hats to church; we should all be wearing crash helmets."[14]

God's miracle-working power is awesome and at times incomprehensible. A common response, when confronted with phenomena akin to the restoration of an infected toe or the resurrection of a dead little girl, is to look for the event's natural cause. How can the miracle, we wonder, be explained in a manner we can understand?

Instead of searching for a natural cause, we should look for a miracle's *intelligent* cause.[15] Underneath the drama and excitement of each miracle lies a careful, thoughtful purpose. Often, one miracle may serve many purposes—such as my sister Jennifer's cancer healing, which made her well, strengthened our faith, and brought glory to God.

The next two sections of this book detail eight purposes for miracles, woven together with a remarkable collection of testimonies to God's power. Catherine Marshall wrote that the Helper "insists upon taking us into the realm of the miraculous."[16] In the coming chapters you will meet people who would understand her sentiments. They have been caught up by God's power. They have experienced His love. And they have benefited from His ability and willingness to intervene in their lives.

They have, to borrow from Dillard's marvelous imagery, exchanged their straw hats for crash helmets.

PART TWO

Power with a Purpose

The Faith Factor

Miracles lead us to faith, and are mainly wrought for the sake of unbelievers.
— A U G U S T I N E

HE CORRELATION BETWEEN MIRACLES AND FAITH is reminiscent of the old "chicken or the egg" question. Which comes first: the miracle or the faith?

The Bible recounts story after story of Christ performing miracles in response to faith. Sometimes, in fact, the Lord seemed to hold His power in check, pending a tangible demonstration of belief. As Herbert Lockyer put it, "Faith was often the condition for which He waited before He could do any mighty work."[1]

Remember the Canaanite woman who had a demon-possessed daughter? She found Jesus hiding out in a friend's home, trying—unsuccessfully—to secure a few moments' peace alone with His disciples away from the crowds that followed Him everywhere. "Have mercy on me, O Lord, Son of David!" the woman cried. "My daughter is severely demon-possessed."

When Jesus failed to respond, she repeated her request—over and over again until the disciples finally grew weary and asked Jesus to deal with her. Turning to the foreign woman, Christ explained the situation: "I was not sent except to the lost sheep of...Israel."

Rejected! Here was the man they called the great Healer, who had gone all over the place performing incredible miracles with seemingly endless compassion, now turning a cold shoulder! At that point, I suspect, most people would have given up getting a miracle and sulked off in broken disappointment or self-righteous anger, thinking, *Who does that Jesus think He is, anyway! Hmph. Maybe demon possession is just too tough for Him. Some miracle worker.*

But not this woman. She was desperate for a miracle—and totally confident in Christ's ability to meet her need. Instead of walking away, she came closer, finally kneeling before the Lord with a simple, reverent plea: "Lord, help me!"

Again, Christ put her off. "It is not good to take the children's bread and throw it to the little dogs."

At this rebuke, the woman had every right to take offense or at least to break down in tears over the Lord's seeming coldheartedness. But here's the kicker: Instead of breaking down, the woman saw a glimmer of hope in Christ's reply and seized on it. "Yes, Lord," she agreed, "yet even the little dogs eat the crumbs which fall from their masters' table."

With that, Christ had heard enough. "O woman, great is your faith!" He exclaimed. "Let it be to you as you desire." And at that moment the woman's daughter was completely healed.[2]

Why did the Lord hold out for so long? Why didn't He just grant the poor woman's request without making her grovel—especially in front of a crowd? Why didn't He show her the compassion He had extended to so many others? Was He simply toying with the woman in an effort to prove He had the upper hand? Or did He refuse her because she was a pagan foreigner?

Christ was not exhibiting unwarranted cruelty; nor was He toying. On the contrary, He restrained His power simply because He recognized the strength of the woman's faith. He did not, according to R. C. Trench, wait an instant longer than was absolutely necessary, and He knew she would emerge victorious from the trial. Moreover, she gained a "mightier and purer faith" than if she had simply received her miracle on demand.[3]

The Canaanite woman received a double blessing. She got her miracle, and her faith grew. Which came first? Christ waited on her faith, to be sure, yet the miracle also *produced* faith—both in the woman and, no doubt, in others who witnessed or heard about the miracle. This pattern—of faith resulting in miracles and miracles producing faith—reveals itself again and again throughout Scripture.

As I interviewed people for this book, the pattern repeated itself. Almost without exception the folks I talked with pointed to faith as the factor that contributed to, or grew out of, their experiences with the miraculous. And in listening to their stories, I learned three distinct lessons about faith: First, God is powerful enough that He *can* do miracles. Next, God loves us enough that He *will* do miracles. And finally, God's power, ability, and love stretch beyond anything we can ask or imagine; these forces know *no limits*.

BELIEVING GOD CAN DO IT

Kevin Casteen started his sprint the moment he saw the snap. He had always been one of the fastest guys on his youth football team, and if he could get open now, he knew he could catch the long bomb and take it in for a touchdown. He pushed harder, willing himself to run, but it was already too late. The defenders were on him, swarming past him, effectively destroying all chances for a score.

Kevin kicked the dirt in frustration. At ten years old he relished the challenge of a hard-fought athletic contest. It felt so good to push the limits of his endurance. Lately, though, those limits had seemed shorter and shorter. Just the other day he had had to almost drag himself up the staircase. How could such a simple thing as going upstairs take so much out of a boy?

As the weeks went by, Kevin got slower and slower. His parents could not help but notice the change in their once-active son. He seemed to be steadily losing strength. Was he just tired, they wondered, or was something seriously wrong?

The Casteens' pediatrician examined Kevin and gave him a clean bill of health. "He's just growing," the doctor said reassuringly "Remember, Kevin will be a teenager soon. You may be in for a lot of changes—but everything looks okay."

But everything was *not* okay. Kevin suffered from an extremely rare muscle disease. Similar to muscular dystrophy, the incurable illness attacks the muscles in its victim, weakening and wasting them until the person is confined to a wheelchair. Even thoughtless movements, such as blinking, become virtually impossible as the disease progresses. Some patients have had to have their eyes taped open to be able to see.

Kevin's symptoms were spotted by another pediatrician, a family friend, who happened to be familiar with the strange disease. The doctor immediately referred Kevin to one of the nation's leading muscle-disease clinics, where a series of tests and a muscle biopsy confirmed the diagnosis. Kevin's muscles were literally breaking down.

A team of specialists recommended steroids to slow the breakdown, yet Kevin's condition continued to worsen. No longer could he enjoy sports such as football and tennis; instead, Kevin looked forward to the times when his friends would come inside and play cards and other quiet games with him. Kevin's doctors could offer little hope; mortality rates were high, and even if the disease went into remission, relapse could occur at any time.

Life presented a new set of challenges. If Kevin happened to fall down at school, for example, he had to be helped to his feet by his classmates. Three times a week he and his parents made the hour-long trek to the clinic, where blood tests monitored the muscle breakdown with grim consistency. Kevin was too young to be seriously frightened—but his parents were desperate for help.

Anne Casteen believed God could heal her son, although she had never known anyone to experience an actual miracle. She had, however, heard about a woman named Kathryn Kuhlman, who was reputed to have a tremendous healing ministry. "You need to go to one of Kuhlman's services," a friend advised. "Try to go to one in Pittsburgh. That's where her regular services are—it'll be easier for you to get in."

The Casteens went to Pittsburgh. Anne arrived at the church at 5:30 A.M.—a good four hours before the service was to start—and secured three of the only seats left. They were in the last row. By the time the service began, the lines of people vying to get into the church stretched around the block.

One of the ushers had been tipped off to the Casteens' presence by a mutual friend. As the service started, she invited the family to move to the front of the sanctuary. Within moments Kuhlman appeared, wearing an orange chiffon evening gown and swooshing her arms before the congregation. Kevin and his parents had not known what to expect. "It was a good thing the usher had put us in the front," he reflected later, "because if we had still been sitting in the back, we would have been out of there."

Kevin's mother had explained to him that this church was special and that people were apt to be healed. It did not seem surprising, then, when the man behind the Casteens got out of his wheelchair and began to walk. Likewise, Kevin watched, with a mixture of acceptance and awe, as a woman's giant goiter disappeared from her neck. One moment, Kevin couldn't help but stare at the protrusion; when he looked again, it was gone.

Watching the crowd, Kevin almost forgot why he and his family had come to the service. His father had warned him not to get his hopes up too high. Suddenly, though, Kevin felt as though someone had poured hot coffee down his back.

Startled, he turned around—yet no one else seemed to have noticed anything unusual. Kevin glanced at his parents. They were praying, he guessed, for him.

It wasn't long before the usher who had befriended the Casteens returned to inquire how Kevin was feeling. When Kevin told her about the warm sensation he had experienced, she asked him to accompany her to the back of the church.

"Is there something in particular you could not do before?" the woman asked.

"Well," Kevin replied, "I can't walk up stairs."

The usher pointed to a small stone stairway leading to the church balcony. "Try going up those steps right there."

Kevin admitted he did not feel any different—but he was willing to give it a try. He walked over to the staircase, and grasping the railing for support, took the first two steps. Then, amazed at his success, he let go of the railing and continued mounting the steps. By the time his father followed him out of the sanctuary, Kevin was trotting up and down the stairs. He turned and saw tears in his father's eyes.

"What else couldn't you do?" the usher pressed.

"I can't get up off the floor by myself," Kevin said. His arms had become so thin and weak he could not support his own weight, even to lift himself to a kneeling position.

Kevin's father helped him get down on the floor and then watched as Kevin slowly pulled himself upright, using the steps for support. The effort was worth it; for the first time in more than a year, Kevin got to his feet without assistance.

"Do you want to go up to the front again and see Miss Kuhlman?" the usher asked. Throughout the service, people who had been healed—like the woman with the goiter—had gone up to the platform to share their stories. Kevin wanted to get a closer look at the dramatic evangelist, and he agreed to go forward.

"How old are you, son?" Kuhlman asked.

"Eleven."

"What was wrong with you?"

Kevin explained about his illness, and he demonstrated the change that had just taken place. As he spoke, he looked at Kuhlman and felt a warmth and love unlike anything he'd ever known. He wanted to stay there on stage with her forever—but she had another question to ask.

"What do you want to do now?"

Kevin answered automatically He had not eaten that day, and he was hungry. "I guess I want to go get a hamburger," he said.

Kuhlman laughed. "Well," she said, "why don't you and your folks just go on and leave now ahead of the crowd."

As Kevin walked out of the church, there was no doubt in his mind. He had been touched by God, and he was healed.

In the months that followed, Kevin's doctors continued to monitor his blood. It had returned to normal, and all evidence of the disease disappeared.

Some time later Kevin had the opportunity to visit the Mayo Clinic, where his miracle was confirmed as the doctors studied Kevin's records and ran additional tests. "You definitely had the disease," they concurred, "but it's gone. We cannot explain it."

Kevin did not need a medical explanation. He knew what had happened— and that was enough. He was happy just to be back on the football field. He had a lot of practicing to do; after all, his first game was only a few weeks away.

Kevin's faith in God's ability to heal set the stage for his miracle. And, true to the pattern of miracles and faith, Kevin's miracle increased his faith. It also opened his eyes to the depth of God's mercy and love—an awareness that is vital to our faith in God's willingness to work miracles.

Believing God Will Do It

Like Kevin Casteen, Aloma Hindman believed in miracles, at least theoretically. She figured God could heal people if He wanted to—but then again, the people in her church who got sick usually wound up dying. Healing, it seemed, wasn't really part of God's modern work. God might be powerful enough to perform miracles, but maybe, Aloma thought, He just wasn't willing to do them.

For years Aloma had undergone routine mammograms. The experience was never a pleasant one, but Aloma had always been healthy and she wanted to keep it that way. She was about to become a grandmother; she couldn't afford to get sick.

Now, sitting in the radiologist's office, she wondered why things were taking more time than usual. They had always given her an on-the-spot report. *What could possibly be taking so long?* Finally, a nurse poked her head into the room. "We need to take one more picture."

Aloma felt her stomach sink. *One more picture.* That could only mean they'd found something. That could only mean problems.

Moments later Aloma's fears were confirmed. The tests revealed two masses, and a subsequent biopsy indicated that the cancer in her breast was malignant. Aloma thought of her grandbaby, so soon to be born, and her thirteen-year-old son. *It's over,* she thought. *I'll never get to hold my first grandchild.*

One of Aloma's favorite books was *A Man Called Peter,* a biography of the late Peter Marshall, a minister. She read the book over and over again and was thrilled to learn that Marshall's son, Peter John, was to conduct a church service in her town. "Do you think Peter would pray for me?" Aloma asked her husband, Roy.

Roy did not know, but he took Aloma to the service. The church was packed, and Aloma began to despair. Afterward, Marshall autographed books, surrounded by a throng of admirers. "Oh, Lord," Aloma cried, "I'll never get to see him."

Suddenly, though, the crowd cleared, and Marshall spotted Aloma and Roy. He seemed to sense their concern. "What's wrong?" he inquired.

Aloma told him about the cancer and said she was terrified of the surgery, scheduled for the coming Thursday.

"You've given up, haven't you?" Marshall softly asked the question to which he already knew the answer. Aloma nodded her head.

Marshall began to pray, rebuking Aloma's fear and asking the Lord for healing. The three of them—Marshall, Aloma, and Roy—stood there praying for twenty-five minutes. Afterward, Aloma felt a marvelous peace.

As the surgery date approached, though, her fears returned, bringing with them vivid nightmares. Why, Aloma wondered, could she not shake her terror?

Finally Thursday came. The operation was over quickly, and Aloma left the hospital the following day. The surgeon had cleaned out her lymph nodes and removed her breast, but Aloma's battle was just beginning. Chemotherapy treatments had to be started immediately.

Aloma dreaded the very idea. Sitting before the mirror in her bedroom, she brushed her thick, dark hair. "Gosh," she thought, "there's so much of it." She wondered how long it would be before she needed to purchase a wig.

Aloma turned to her Bible for comfort. Faith, she read, comes by hearing God's Word.[4] To combat her fears and build her faith, Aloma surrounded herself with books and tapes designed to saturate her consciousness with the promises of Scripture. Still, she could not dismiss the feeling that she was a bad person, that perhaps God did not really love her, and that she somehow deserved to be sick.

A few weeks later Aloma accompanied her husband on a business trip. Returning to their hotel room one evening, she discovered a note on her bed:

Aloma—
 God loves you very much. Keep fighting the good fight of faith.

—Your Maid,
 Roberta

Aloma could not believe her eyes. Obviously, the maid had seen her name inscribed on the jacket of her Bible—but how could she have known that Aloma was struggling with her faith?

Aloma searched the hotel until she found the housekeeper who had cleaned her room. The woman confessed that when she entered Aloma's room she had gotten goosebumps. She knew the Lord was at work, and she began to pray. God, she said, had prompted her to leave the note on the bed.

Aloma read the words over and over again. *God loves you very much.* Never before had she recognized or been so convinced of God's love and acceptance. Suddenly, she realized something she hadn't understood before: God was more than simply able to heal her. He *loved* her, and—dared she even hope it?—He was *willing* to give her a miracle.

Aloma did not have long to wait.

Roy sensed the miracle first, about a month after Aloma's chemotherapy ended. Driving along the highway one night, he was praying for Aloma when three words pierced his thoughts: *Aloma is healed.* He continued to pray, and again the message came: *Aloma is healed.* Roy knew God had spoken to him, and he could not wait to share the good news with his wife.

Sure enough, at Aloma's next checkup the oncologist could find nothing wrong with her blood.

What Aloma did not know was that the treatment she received was typically reserved for the most dire cancer cases—patients the doctors did not expect to live very long. The chemo helped fight the cancer, but unfortunately, in the process it almost always damaged a patient's joints and organs. It was an unpleasant trade but one the doctors felt had to be made.

When Aloma's bloodwork continued to show no traces of cancer, the doctors finally stopped the treatment. Miraculously, it had done no damage to her joints or organs—and Aloma began to enjoy a regular jogging program. Her hair, however, was totally gone.

To Aloma, such a consequence mattered little. She knew the hair would grow back eventually. In the meantime, she had found a perfectly suitable wig—and her precious new baby granddaughter, snuggled contentedly in her grandmother's arms, did not seem to mind it at all.

Once we realize, as Aloma did, that God loves us enough to do miracles on our behalf, faith takes on a whole new dimension. This understanding of God's love and compassion, paired with a belief in God's power to work miracles, pushes the boundaries of what He can do beyond anything we could ever ask or imagine.

BELIEVING GOD'S POWER KNOWS NO LIMITS

Larry Dantzler believed in miracles. He had seen them firsthand, and he knew God was willing and able to meet people's needs in a modern world. What he did not fully recognize was just how powerful—and even unpredictable—God's intervention could be.

Larry loved to participate in the crusades his church, under the auspices of International Evangelistic Ministries, sponsored in various corners of the world. Experiencing new cultures, meeting new people, and seeing the response of those who had never known God's love made each missions trip dynamic and exciting. Best of all, Larry welcomed the demonstration of God's power that typically accompanied the services. The sermons were always very simple, but the miracles that followed were amazing.

On this trip they were in Lagos, Nigeria, a country dominated by Muslims. As Larry and his team members prepared for the evening service, he reflected on the incredible events he had witnessed. Crippled people walked, deaf people could hear, and the blind received their sight. All manner of miracles were apt to take place during a typical crusade, and Larry anticipated that this night would be no different.

The previous services had been well attended. A number of dramatic hearings had occurred—which meant that more people would be back tonight. Crowds were already gathering in the open field where the meetings took place. The music started, and Larry looked forward to telling the throng about Jesus and the power of God.

After the messages were delivered by Larry and his team members, the audience was invited to accept Jesus, followed by a mass prayer for the sick. Then a number of Nigerians who had personally experienced God's power got up to share their stories. The air was electric with anticipation. This, the crowd knew, was the moment for miracles.

Suddenly Larry saw an older man walking toward him. He recognized the fellow from an earlier service in which the man had converted to Christianity. This time the man brought a girl of about seven or eight, whom he introduced as his granddaughter. "Will you pray for her?" he asked Larry.

Larry smiled. "Sure!" he replied—and then he saw the little girl's arm.

It was totally shriveled and deformed, locked into a grotesque angle by her side. Larry stared at the useless appendage.

"Jesus will heal my granddaughter." It was not a question, but more of a statement, delivered by a man who, just two days earlier, had made a monumental decision to renounce his Muslim heritage in favor of Christianity. Larry felt his faith draining away.

He was far less certain than the Nigerian grandfather. All of the other hearings had been *en masse*, the work of a seemingly indiscriminate power hovering over the crowd. In contrast, this man wanted prayer for a specific problem—and what a problem it was! Larry had never seen such a grossly disfigured arm. But there was nothing to do, he realized, except pray.

Larry closed his eyes. "Father," he prayed, "touch this little girl tonight." *What happens,* Larry wondered, *if God doesn't show up?* Afraid to look, Larry continued to pray.

His prayer grew longer and longer. Larry realized he sounded convincing—but still, he refused to open his eyes. He sensed, rather than saw, that a crowd had gathered to watch. How much longer should he pray before wrapping things up? Was there any way to get out of this situation without damaging the new convert's faith? How could he explain things to the disappointed onlookers?

All at once, Larry heard a tremendous shout. He stopped praying and opened his eyes. There, standing before him with both of her arms raised high in the air, was the little girl. Her arms were a perfect match—both totally normal, straight, and whole. The crowd was filled with excitement and praise as the girl continued to display her new arm.

Larry smiled. The Nigerians could see he was happy. They could never know, however, the depth of his amazement and gratitude. He had learned an invaluable lesson that day: God's power knows no limits. It is bigger than our expectations, bigger than our hopes, and bigger than our faith.

Larry had discovered for himself what the Canaanite woman with the demonized daughter had known all along: *Nothing is impossible with God.*

Overcoming Obstacles

*Faith leads us to employ our God-given
talents in God's service.*

—WILLIAM BENNETT

IRACLES, AS WE SAW IN THE LAST CHAPTER, both respond to and produce faith. Yet they also have a supremely practical function, one that is tangible, useful, and even—in some cases—essential for the effective fulfillment of our responsibilities and goals.

God uses miracles to remove or circumvent the things that stand in the way of ministry and work. By overcoming these obstacles, miracles reveal God's commitment to His servants: When He gives us a job to do, we can count on Him to make a way—even if the task at hand seems impossible.

The account of Peter's mother-in-law reveals God's eye for meeting our needs in a practical manner. Apparently she lived with Peter and his wife, because when Peter brought Jesus and some of the other fellows home with him one day, there she was, sick in bed with a fever.

I imagine Peter and his friends, like today's Sunday brunchers, were hungry that day. They had all gone straight to Peter's house when the synagogue let out—expecting, I think, to continue their fellowship over a satisfying meal.

Instead, the hearth was cold. The table was bare.

The boys could have rustled up some sandwiches, but they had a better idea. "Hey, Jesus," they said, "Peter's mother-in-law isn't feeling too great. We think she has a fever. Will You take a look at her?"

I love the powerful simplicity of Christ's response. He went to the woman, took her hand, and helped her up. The fever left her, and she began to wait on them.[1]

Jesus saw a need and met it. There was work to be done, and the situation called for a miracle. It's a story that reminds me of a modern-day miracle that happened in a small Korean village....

THE DEACONESS THEY COULDN'T DO WITHOUT

Sung Ryong Kwak scanned the crowd with the practiced eye of a veteran evangelist. Whenever his church sponsored an evangelism program, Sung signed up to help. This time, he noticed, the response to the campaign was better than anyone had anticipated. The seven-hundred-member congregation had planned thirteen services on one Sunday to accommodate the ten thousand people who had been invited. Looking out over the throng, Sung could tell that at least that many had responded. Follow-up work would be a challenge—but that was a problem Sung and the other campaign planners were happy to have.

For the next month Sung and his fellow team members met daily to recap their ministry results and pray for their ongoing contact work. They wanted to meet with everyone who had attended the services. One night, just before midnight, the telephone rang. One of Sung's friends answered it. When he rejoined the group, his face bore a somber expression.

"Lee is in the hospital," he said. "There was carbon monoxide in her room—the doctors are trying to resuscitate her now."

Sung exchanged a concerned look with another team leader. Lee was a deaconess in their church, and she served as one of the chief coordinators for the evangelistic teams. Without her help, the follow-up work could become an administrative nightmare.

"Let's go." Under the dark skies, Sung and the others made their way to the small hospital in their village. A knot of people had already gathered outside the emergency room, including the pastor of Sung's church and several elders. As they prayed for Lee's survival, the medical team tried repeatedly to jump-start her heart. Like a circuit breaker being turned on and off, the defibrillator machine worked to reset the natural rhythm of Lee's heart. "Please, Lord," Sung prayed, "let it start beating again."

Hrumph. Over and over again Sung could see the doctors using the machine to shock the life back into Lee's body. It was no good; the heart monitor showed a solitary, flat line. After more than an hour of trying, the chief doctor finally made a decision. "The patient is dead," he said. Turning to the group from Sung's church, he told them to begin making funeral arrangements.

Sung felt numb. As his friends silently shuffled out of the room, he wanted to cry out. *No! Lee cannot die! Lord, don't You know how much we need her?*

Sung needed to be alone with the Lord. He knew Lee had been declared dead, but he wanted, more than anything, to pray for his friend.

Sung found a quiet corner in the hospital. "Lord," he prayed, "please give life to this lady once more. This is a crucial time for our evangelistic ministry. Lee's death will affect our entire village.

"Lord, we need a miracle."

As Sung continued to pray, a passage of Scripture etched itself into his mind: *I am the resurrection and the life. He who believes in Me, though he may die, he shall live.*[2] Sung repeated the verses over and over again. Hours passed—and then, suddenly, Sung knew that something was going to happen. He got up and ran to his church.

Breathless, Sung burst through the door. There stood Lee's family, quietly making plans for her funeral with the pastor. Unwilling to raise their hopes with the seemingly idiotic belief that Lee might yet be alive, Sung kept his feelings to himself. He made his way to a prayer room, where he continued to intercede on Lee's behalf. Finally, he could stand it no longer. He returned to the hospital to see whether a miracle had, in fact, taken place.

Lee was nowhere to be found.

Sung's heart sank. *They must have taken her to the morgue*, he reasoned. Dejected, he decided to go back to the church. Leaving the hospital, he almost bumped into a young intern. Sung recognized the girl as a member of the medical team that had tried to help save Lee's life.

Before Sung could ask any questions, the girl spoke. "They took her to the big hospital," she said. Sung was confused; the main hospital was in the city. That was more than thirty minutes away—why would the doctors send a dead person there?

"I couldn't help but notice you and your friends," the intern explained. "I was impressed by your prayers, and after you left, I persuaded the doctor to try and shock the woman's heart one more time. He did—and her heartbeat returned. They transferred her to the big hospital."

Sung was elated. When he reached the main hospital, though, his joy turned to concern. Lee was alive, but the medical staff told him she would probably be severely handicapped as a result of the carbon-monoxide poisoning. After all, she was more than sixty years old. Brain damage, or some other crippling problem, was a virtual certainty.

Three days later Sung got the surprise of his life. He was sitting in church when Lee walked, unassisted, through the door. She was in perfect health!

Lee smiled purposefully at Sung. He returned the greeting, knowing what was on her mind: There was work to be done, people to visit, teams to coordinate.

Sung breathed a sigh of relief. With Lee back on the job, the ministry would be efficient, effective, and powerful.

The story of Lee's resurrection makes perfect sense to readers interested in the intelligent cause, or purpose, behind miracles: Sung and his team needed Lee's know-how and leadership in order to carry their evangelism efforts through to completion. Skeptical readers, however, will look for the natural explanation. Perhaps the small village hospital had antiquated monitors and equipment, or maybe the chief doctor lacked the professional expertise of his counterparts in more "advanced" societies and therefore failed to recognize the signs of life when he declared the deaconess dead.

Eight hundred years ago, during the Middle Ages, no such questions would have been raised. People may have wondered as to the whys and why nots of divine intervention, but miracles themselves were generally accepted as an integral part of ordinary life.[3] The largest collection of miracles for the period centers around a twelfth-century saint, Thomas Becket—the "holy blisful martir" we recognize in Chaucer's *Canterbury Tales*.

SAINT THOMAS AND THE PRIEST WHO COULDN'T TALK

Becket served as the archbishop of Canterbury. He was murdered in his cathedral in 1170—an event that immediately elevated him to the status of martyr and spawned more than seven hundred miracles associated with his name during the next fifteen years. Canterbury became the dominant shrine of the period, a place where the sick came to be cured and where pilgrims—such as Chaucer's merry band—offered thanksgiving for cures that had happened elsewhere in the name of Saint Thomas.[4]

All manner of healings manifested themselves. As one observer put it at the time, "paralytics are cured, the blind see, the deaf hear, the dumb speak, the lame walk, lepers are cured...and (a thing unheard of from the days of our fathers) the dead are raised."⁵ The monks took great care to record each miracle carefully and without exaggeration, not to forestall skepticism but to protect themselves. Becket had impious enemies in high places—including those who had assisted in his murder—and there were those who stood ready to intimidate and arrest any who spoke well of the martyr or magnified his miracles.⁶

Always on the lookout for charlatans and other impostors, the monks were known to reject miracles that lacked sufficient proof or corroborating witnesses. One story that passed their test concerns a priest from London who had lost his ability to speak. The priest saw, in a vision, that if his tongue were touched with the archbishop's blood, he would be able to talk again. This notion must have seemed odd to the priest, since at that time Thomas was, as far as he knew, alive and in good health.

Nevertheless, when the same vision was repeatedly revealed to one of the priest's friends, the two of them decided to make the trek to Canterbury. As they approached the city, imagine their surprise: The city was in an uproar; the archbishop had just been murdered!

This news served to strengthen the men's faith, and they lost no time in making their way to the cathedral. There they begged for a few drops of the martyr's blood. The request was not as strange as it might seem. Miracles were known to be associated with the blood of a martyr, and even as Thomas's body was lying on the pavement where he had been slain, people scrambled to collect his blood in little vials or dip their clothing into it. The atmosphere was one of general confusion.⁷

Somehow in the melee the London priest secured a bit of the blood for himself. He touched it to his tongue, and immediately, the report maintains, "it was loosed." The miracle was confirmed by many witnesses—people who afterward heard the priest celebrate mass.⁸

Therein, to me, lies the story's punch line. It was no secret that many who were cured at Canterbury turned a profit on their experience, using their miracle to beg for alms. The priest's condition had been well known; he certainly could have made his livelihood as one of the "living miracles of Canterbury"— precursors, in a sense, to today's sideshow freaks. Instead, the man returned to his pulpit and continued his ministry. The obstacle to his service—his inability to talk—had been graciously and practically removed.

CALLED TO SERVE

The priest's miracle was, again, only one of hundreds that were recorded at the time. It is not the most amazing story nor the most well-known of the Canterbury miracles. It appealed to me, however, because it reveals how naturally and beautifully miracles dovetail with service. The account of Peter's mother-in-law is not the only scriptural precedent for this match; Tabitha was raised from the dead and presumably continued her selfless devotion to meeting the needs of others, and Epaphroditus saw his health restored and then ministered to Paul and the Philippian church. Even the miraculous gifts, Paul says, are to be used in order to edify people.[9]

Paul would have loved Connie and Geoff Griffith. Missionaries in Africa, they were committed to sowing love, hope, and joy as they brought light to a darkened world. Geoff had been working with Hindu people when the couple decided to travel to India to observe firsthand the ministry taking place in that country.

Aboard a train bound from New Delhi to a small village in southern India, Connie focused on the trip ahead. She and Geoff planned to visit and work with another missionary couple who ran two orphanages in southern India. The train trip would take thirty-eight hours. Connie had been warned not to eat the food on the train, and surveying her grimy surroundings, she could understand the admonition.

Contemplating the Indian orphans, Connie's thoughts wandered to her own two daughters, ages six and eight. She and Geoff had left them in the care of some friends in Africa, and she hoped the children would behave themselves. They had only been gone for a few days, but already Connie longed to see her girls again.

As day turned into night and then into day again, Connie began to wish she and Geoff had thought to bring more food along. She was famished. How bad could the train food possibly be, she wondered.

"Geoff," she said finally, "I'm starving. I'd rather take my chances with the food on this train than faint from starvation before we ever get to the orphanage. Let's get some dinner."

Geoff agreed, and Connie selected curried mutton from the limited menu. It wasn't long before she regretted her choice; the meat was spoiled and Connie's stomach began to rebel. She spent the rest of the train ride weaving her way to the bathroom.

"Thank goodness," Connie mumbled when the train finally stopped. Her relief, however, was short-lived as Geoff steered her toward a bus that would take them to the village that served as home to the first orphanage. Elbowing her way through the crowd on the bus, Connie lost sight of her husband. He was nearby, she knew, but she could not see him. Instead, she found herself all but crushed by the weight of a drunk as he sat down beside her and promptly passed out on her shoulder.

By the time the bus arrived in the village, Connie felt almost delirious. She had to get some fresh air. She stepped down from the bus and was met by a blast of heat. Shielding her eyes from the blazing sun, Connie picked up her suitcase and hoisted it, African-style, on top of her head.

"Honey, are you okay?" Geoff sounded concerned.

"I'll be fine," Connie assured him. "I just need to walk a bit."

The walk turned into a hike as the Griffiths made their way toward the orphanage. They had been invited for dinner, and when they finally arrived, exhausted, Connie sank gratefully into her chair. Dinner was served.

Suddenly, Connie's stomach flip-flopped. A family of rats had apparently made its home in the rafters above the dining area, and now, as Connie watched, their droppings fell onto her plate. Connie excused herself and retreated to her bedroom.

Later, Geoff came in. "Connie," he asked again, "are you all right?"

"I feel awful," Connie admitted.

"I'm supposed to be gone all day tomorrow," Geoff said, "but I don't want to leave you like this."

"I'll be okay. I think I just need some rest." Connie seldom got sick, and she was sure she would be up and about the next day.

When morning came, Geoff slipped noiselessly out of bed. Connie seemed to be sleeping peacefully, but Geoff wanted to alert their missionary hosts to keep an eye on her.

For Connie, the next three days were a blur. Geoff traveled during the day, returning to check on her at night. The missionaries, thinking Connie had been undone by the miserable poverty of their surroundings, left her alone to recuperate. When the time finally came to move on to the second orphanage, Connie struggled to her feet.

When the missionaries saw their guest, they were aghast. "You are sick!" the wife exclaimed.

"Yes," Connie agreed, "I've been in the bathroom for the past three days."

"Oh!" the missionaries cried in dismay. "We thought you couldn't stand being here, and we figured you didn't want to be bothered! You look awful—you'll never make it to the other orphanage. We need to get you to a hospital."

Too weak to disagree, Connie allowed Geoff to lift her into the missionaries' jeep. The missionary couple clambered into the vehicle, and the group began the three-hour drive to the nearest hospital.

Fifteen minutes into the ride, Connie's muscles began to cramp. First her fingers then her knees and toes curled inward. Finally she found herself paralyzed, sitting like a little perched bird in the back of the jeep as it bounced along the primitive road.

"She's not going to make it," the missionary wife said, beginning to cry.

Oh for pity's sake, Connie thought, *nobody dies from dehydration!* Then, as the trip wore on, her condition worsened. Her lips pulled back from her teeth. Geoff's face reflected shock as he stared at his wife's horrible grimace.

"God," he cried, "please do a miracle! *Do something!*"

Dimly, Connie heard her husband's plea. Her thoughts were far off in Africa, with her precious daughters. *God,* she thought, *I've got two little girls. If I die, I don't know how they'll adjust or manage.*

Suddenly the missionary who was driving the jeep let out a shout. "Look," he cried, "it's the Red Cross!" Sure enough, just off the old trail was a small white building that bore the red mark of the international relief association. No other buildings were in sight.

As the jeep pulled to a stop, Connie tried to protest. The AIDS epidemic was all too familiar in these remote areas, and Connie knew it was common practice to reuse hypodermic needles. "No injection!" she said through clenched teeth, realizing even as she spoke that no one could understand her words.

The group made its way into the brightly lit building, and Connie felt reassured by the facility's cleanliness. An Indian man, dressed in a neat white shirt and baggy pants, greeted the missionaries. He spoke perfect English.

"I know what's wrong with her," he said, motioning to Connie. "She's dehydrated. I have some electrolytes here in this packet. This water has already been boiled." With no further explanation, the stranger mixed the electrolytes and the water and handed Geoff an eye dropper encased in a plastic bag. "It's *sterile,*" he said, looking right at Connie.

The stranger's instructions were clear: Geoff was to feed Connie one drop at a time until they reached the hospital. Connie's mouth had locked open, and as the group set off again in the jeep, Geoff began the slow process of rehydrating Connie's body.

An hour and a half later the group arrived at the hospital. Connie had swallowed a good bit of the medicine, and her muscles had relaxed. She was able to walk into the hospital by herself.

Even so, the Indian doctor who examined Connie expressed concern. "This is one of the most severe cases of dehydration I've seen," she said. "Your body has sucked the water out of the cells. It is surprising you don't have damage in your kidneys or your heart. You came within hours of dying."

Connie stayed in the hospital for three days, nourished by IVs as she regained her strength. Finally the doctors released her, and she and Geoff resumed their itinerary by visiting the second orphanage.

A few weeks after their return to Africa, Connie and Geoff received a letter from the missionary couple in India. "You won't believe this," the couple wrote, "but when we returned to our village via the route we had taken to get you to the hospital, that Red Cross building was gone. There is nothing there in the place where it was."

Connie knew her life had been miraculously spared. Catching her daughters in her arms, she thanked God for allowing her to fulfill her service as a wife and missionary and as a mother to her two darling girls.

Fifteen years have passed since Connie's miraculous encounter. She and Geoff still work with the Africa Evangelical Fellowship through the ministry's American office, and they occasionally hear other stories of divine intervention in everyday affairs. Reflecting on her miracle, Connie says that it revealed God's kindness. "It showed me that He cares, that He knows exactly where we are, and that He cannot help but reach out and show us His love from time to time."

God does care about us. Even as He works miracles to build faith and remove things that hinder ministry and service, God is fully aware of our other needs. The Bible says, in fact, that He knows our needs even before we ask Him, and as we will discover in the next chapter, He often uses miracles to meet them.

Help Is on the Way

Your Father knows what you need before you ask.
He is already there. He is in charge of the situation.

—ELISABETH ELLIOT

ANDY MARTIN STARED AT THE CEILING and tried not to feel sorry for herself. Barely a month ago she had been in California, pursuing an acting career. She had landed a film agent—an accomplishment in itself—and, at twenty-six years old, Sandy sensed that her future was full of promise.

But now those memories felt like part of another life, another era. Like a knockout blow from an unseen attacker, mononucleosis had landed Sandy flat on her back and sent her home to her folks' house in Ohio. It was bad enough to be missing the career opportunities of a lifetime, Sandy thought; the fact that she felt too sick and tired to even climb out of bed only added insult to injury.

Sandy heard her mother's footsteps in the hall. "Honey," her mom called, "are you awake?"

Sandy turned her head as her mother entered her room. "Hi, Mom," she managed weakly.

"We prayed for you at my Bible study this morning. One of the ladies recommended a specialist in West Virginia. You don't seem to be getting any better, and I thought maybe we should go see this doctor."

Sandy agreed. She was not, however, prepared for the news the specialist offered: Sandy had Epstein-Barr virus, a potentially fatal infection.

As the disease progressed, Sandy manifested many of the classic symptoms. She developed hard, yellowish lumps on her neck. Her liver swelled painfully, and she could no longer fit into her clothes. Even in loose-fitting garments the pain in her abdomen made it difficult for Sandy to sit up. The worst part, though, was the incredible, endless fatigue. Unable to get out of bed some days, Sandy grew weaker and weaker as the months became a year and then two. Her muscles atrophied until finally she was hardly able to walk.

"It was terrible," she recalls. "I felt like I was always falling down a hill. It was like having a car but no gas."

Then, too, the sickness preyed on Sandy's mind. Once, when she felt well enough to drive, she ran a quick errand—only to find that the disease had "erased" her memory and she could not find her way home. *How long,* Sandy wondered, *can I go on living like this?*

Sandy believed in miracles—in fact, she had researched hundreds of them for a television special on the subject. But would God heal her? She certainly needed His help; the doctors, it seemed, could do little to alleviate her pain or cure the disease. Even so, Sandy was not convinced the Lord would heal her.

Then one day she learned that one of her father's friends, a pastor, planned to conduct a healing service near Sandy's home. Uncertain as to whether she should attend, Sandy prayed.

If you go, came the answer, *you will be healed.*

Sandy knew that God had spoken to her heart. She also knew enough about miracles from her research to know that, in some services, things could get a bit overwhelming. She wondered what to expect.

As the service began, Sandy appreciated the joyful yet reverent attitude of the crowd. When the invitation came, she went to the front of the church, where a line of people waited to be prayed for by the pastor. Finally, it was her turn.

Sandy felt the pastor put his hand on her forehead as he prayed. Then, almost before she knew it, the prayer was over. Sandy looked up. There had been no warm feelings, no rushing lights, none of the drama and excitement she thrived on as an actress—and none of the signs she expected to experience on her own.

"Oh no!" she glumly berated herself. "I should have fallen down—or something."

Disappointed, Sandy turned to walk back to her seat. Out of habit, she placed her hand on her stomach, trying—instinctively—to hide the large, pregnancy-like swelling beneath her clothes. The swelling was gone. *Her stomach was flat!*

Sandy's hand shot to her neck where the ugly yellow lumps had been. *Nothing!* Her neck felt smooth and clean. Awestruck by God's mercy, Sandy could not wait to tell her mother the good news.

Together, they visited Sandy's doctor. After examining her, the physician agreed there were no longer any symptoms of the virus. "The disease is not active," the doctor said. Sandy knew her illness was more than just "not active." It was gone.

Today, Sandy's acting career is back on track. She recently won roles on television's *Matlock* and in the upcoming film *Forgiven*, and she enjoys frequent commercial work. She also teaches acting on the graduate level and has just launched a performing arts school. Looking back, she realizes God used her illness to bring her out of California at a time when her driving ambition to succeed threatened her judgment. Now she is content to let God direct her steps because she understands—from experience—that He knows her needs and exactly how to meet them.

THE PRACTICAL PURPOSE FOR MIRACLES

Elisabeth Elliot, a popular author and radio host, would appreciate Sandy's perspective. "What God gives in answer to our prayers will always be the thing we most urgently need, and it will always be sufficient," she wrote.[1]

God's sufficiency in meeting the needs of men is nothing new. From the very first books of the Old Testament we see God attending to the practical needs of His people—often using miracles in the process. For example, after their dramatic flight out of Egypt—an escape brimming with miracles—the Israelites wandered through the desert for forty years. At one point, after about thirty-eight years, the Israelites found themselves without water. Hot, tired, and thirsty, they began to complain to Moses, their leader.

"Why did you bring us out here to die?" they charged. "This is a terrible place! Nothing can grow on this awful land. And not only that, there is nothing for us to drink!"

Moses went out to talk to God. But before he could say a word, God issued a command. He told Moses to gather the people together. "Speak to the rock before their eyes, and it will yield its water," the Lord promised. "Thus you shall bring water for them out of the rock, and give drink to the congregation and their animals."

Instead of speaking to the rock as God had told him to, Moses struck it with his staff. Yet in spite of this disobedience, God recognized the Israelites' immediate need, and He worked a miracle. Water gushed out of the rock, and everybody had plenty to drink.[2]

"In all times," wrote one French historian, "the supernatural or unexpected emergence of a spring has been considered as a miracle with a practical purpose in view. The spring has a meaning, it answers a need."[3] When the spring appeared in Lourdes, the townsfolk immediately converted it into a pool, and as we saw in chapter 2, the place served as a kind of magnet for the sick and dying. Suffering people, desperate for help, saw in Lourdes a miraculous—and thoroughly practical—answer to their needs.

One marvelous example of the pragmatic purposes in many of the miracles at Lourdes concerns a baby boy named Louis-Justin Bouhohorts. Just eighteen months old, Louis-Justin suffered from terrifying seizures, high fevers, and complete paralysis of his legs. He could not stand or even sit up. His attacks got worse and worse until finally the doctor could do nothing to help. "It is only a matter of hours," he said to the child's parents one day.

Mrs. Bouhohorts reached into the crib to help her dying child.

"Let him alone," the boy's father said. "Can't you see he is very nearly dead?"

Mrs. Bouhohorts refused to concede defeat. When her husband left to make funeral arrangements, she snatched the baby out of his crib and ran to the spring at Lourdes, dug only days before. The water was icy cold, but Mrs. Bouhohorts did not hesitate. She plunged the child in up to his neck and held him there for fifteen minutes. (A doctor, on the scene to observe the happenings at Lourdes, clocked the event.)

Finally, Mrs. Bouhohorts lifted her son out of the pool, bundled him up, and took him home. His body was lifeless and blue, and when Mr. Bouhohorts saw the child, he exploded. "Are you happy now?" he asked. "Have you finished killing him?"

Mrs. Bouhohorts ignored her husband and knelt to pray beside the baby's crib. Within moments she thought she detected some movement. *Could it be?*

"Look," she whispered to her husband, "he is breathing!"

Little Louis-Justin *was* breathing. He spent a peaceful night in bed and awoke to eat a hearty breakfast. As was her custom, his mother returned the boy to his crib while she put away the dishes and tidied up the house.

A few minutes later she heard a strange noise. Was it—*footsteps?* Mrs. Bouhohorts turned and could scarcely believe her eyes. There stood her baby boy—a child who had never walked a day in his life—toddling toward her! He had climbed out of his crib and was walking, just like a normal eighteen-month-old child!

Word spread, and it was not long before the child's doctor arrived. Unable to accept the miracle at first sight, he checked his notes. "I examined this child three days ago," he said. "No change at that time. I wrote here: Still paralysis of the thighs.' I gave him twelve hours to live. And here he is—*walking!*"

Louis-Justin Bouhohorts experienced one of the very first miracles at Lourdes. But his story does not end there. Seventy-five years later, in 1933, Bouhohorts was one of the honored guests at the canonization ceremony for Saint Bernadette, the woman who, as a young girl, scratched the earth to bring forth the miraculous spring at Lourdes.[4]

MEETING BIG—AND LITTLE—NEEDS

Not all miracles, however practical or timely, are as dramatic as the healings that have been documented at Lourdes. Yet, as Jamie Buckingham—the fellow we met in chapter 2 who stabbed himself with a screwdriver—pointed out, there are "no big miracles and little miracles. All miracles are big—for they reflect the nature of our big God....They reveal a God who not only created nature, but who still controls it by the higher law of love."[5]

I experienced this loving provision firsthand not long after Virginia, our third daughter, was born. The late afternoon shadows were just beginning to dance across our queen-size bed as I nursed the baby for what seemed like the twenty-eighth time that day. I would like to say I watched the shadows play and mused over how the precious bundle I held in my arms would one day dance lightly too—but this was not an afternoon for musing. I was exhausted.

As four-year-old Hillary climbed onto the bed, my tired mind catalogued the various fairy tales and Bible stories I knew. Which one, I wondered, would require the least amount of mental effort on my part and still keep Hillary entertained while I finished feeding Virginia?

But Hillary surprised me. She didn't want a story; instead, she simply pointed to my diamond-and-sapphire engagement ring. "Did Daddy give that to you?" she asked, knowing already the answer.

"Yes."

"What for?"

"Because he loves me."

"Can I wear it?"

Having won a reprieve from storytelling, I agreed. "But you have to stay right here and play with it on the bed," I said.

That was the last thing I remember. When I awoke, the room was almost dark. *How long have I been asleep?* I looked down at little Virginia, dozing contentedly. Where, I wondered, was Hillary? And, more immediately, where was my ring?

I ran my fingers across the white coverlet. Nothing. I shook out the pillows and felt underneath the baby. Softly, but with determination, I eased myself off the bed, flipped on the light, and began a systematic search. The ring was not on the bed or the floor. Had Hillary put it on the dresser? No. In my jewelry box? No. In her jewelry box? No.

I found Hillary in the basement playroom, serving make-believe tea to her younger sister Annesley and watching a *Barney* rerun. "Hillary," I asked, "where's Mommy's ring?"

"Ummm. I don't know."

I stood in front of the television set. "Think, Hillary. Did you put it in your room? Do you remember wearing it downstairs? Did you take it off?"

Lamely, Hillary offered what few suggestions her four-year-old mind could conjure. I followed her advice, enthusiastically at first but with growing despair as I realized she had no idea where she'd left the ring.

I decided to pray. "Lord," I said simply, "I need Your help. Show me where to look."

Knowing Hillary could not have gone outside, I resolved to search every inch of our home. I began in the bedroom again—noting, with relief, that the baby was still asleep. Next, I tried all of Hillary's favorite pack-rat stores: dresser drawers, shoe boxes, backpacks, doll cases, teacups, and bookbags. I turned up an interesting assortment of long-forgotten trinkets, but no engagement ring.

Finally, I returned to the playroom. Standing next to our child-sized playhouse, I was about to resolicit Hillary's useless input when a scrap from a lollipop wrapper caught my eye. It was peeking out from the crack where the wall meets the carpet, all but hidden behind the playhouse. I picked it up, and as I did so, something sparkled.

Could it be? I reached down and poked my finger into the crack. I felt the scrape of a carpet tack. But something else was there. I tugged at the rug, wrenching the tacks out of the floor, and then I saw it: a half-moon of gold tucked underneath the baseboard of the basement wall. There was a space less than a quarter of an inch deep where the wall hung above the floor, and it was into this crevice that my ring had turned. The gemstones were concealed beneath the wall.

I had to work to get the ring loose. How it had gotten wedged under the wall—beneath the rug—I can only imagine: Our girls like to climb atop the playhouse, and the ring must have slipped off Hillary's finger and fallen down between the house and the playroom wall, dropping through the crack and somehow turning a corner upon hitting the floor to slide underneath the wall. No four-year-old human hand could have put it there—the jab of the carpet tacks would have thwarted any such effort. The odds against my ring hiding in such an obscure place were tremendous—*almost* as impossible, I realized, as the chances of my ever finding the ring. God, I knew, had shown me exactly where to look.

To some, my experience may not constitute a miracle in the most proper sense of the word. A friend of mine prefers to call such anecdotes "God is real" stories. But isn't that, in itself, a miracle: that God would intervene in a seemingly trivial matter—and there is absolutely no doubt in my mind that He did, in fact, intervene—simply to show Himself *real*?

I believe that R. C. Trench, who served as archbishop of Dublin during the nineteenth century, would have accepted my point of view. He wrote of a miracle's ability to claim the attention of certain men, speaking to them in particular, singling them out from the multitude.[6] Admitting that there were indeed things that could be explained according to the course of nature, Trench made a case for describing an event—such as the discovery of my ring—as miraculous:

> AT THE SAME TIME the finger of God may be so plainly discernible in it that even while it is plainly explicable by natural causes, we yet may be entirely justified in terming it a miracle, a *providential*, although not an absolute, miracle. Absolute it cannot be called, since there were known causes [the lollipop wrapper, for example] perfectly capable of bringing it about. Yet the natural may in a manner lift itself up into the miraculous, by the moment at which it falls out, by the purposes which it is made to fulfil. It is a subjective wonder, a wonder *for us*, though not an objective, not a wonder in itself.[7]

To paraphrase the archbishop, when it comes to defining the miraculous, *timing* is everything. That, and *purpose*. Writing this book, I have been party to countless stories that testify to God's incredible sense of timing and purpose in meeting our specific needs. One such report concerns an Australian couple, Rae and Tony McClellan.

Perfect Timing

Rae looked across the dinner table at the well-to-do couple she and Tony had met at church. Steve and Marlene seemed nice enough, and when they had invited the McClellans out to dinner, Tony and Rae had readily agreed. The two couples seemed to have a lot in common—but now, sitting in the restaurant, Rae realized how different their lives probably were.

Tony and Rae were no strangers to prosperity. Living in London, they had frequented weekend parties in places like Monte Carlo, where they mingled easily with the world's social elite. Business had been brisk in their software company—until one day a deal went sour and the McClellans had watched in stunned dismay as their software went into escrow and all their holdings disappeared, literally overnight.

Rae's attention returned to the dinner conversation. Marlene was asking Tony how business was going.

"How's business?" Tony laughed. "It's awful. It's like hitting my head against a brick wall."

Tony was smiling, but Rae knew that behind the bravado lay genuine concern. Business *was* awful. She and Tony had been careful with their spending, but bills had to be paid, and on more than one occasion they had come to the end of their resources. Just last week, in fact, she and Tony had received word from their daughter's school that, unless her fees were paid within seven days, she would not be allowed to sit for her final exams and would be unable to graduate. They needed three thousand dollars. Rae wondered what they would have done if a friend had not called, out of the blue, and provided that exact amount. The gift—unsolicited, unexpected, and so generous—had overwhelmed the McClellans. God had provided a miracle.

But now Steve was speaking. "I hate to ask this," he said, "but do you need money?"

Tony smiled again. "No, thank you. We did last Monday—in fact, we were desperate. We needed to make the final payment for Samantha's schooling, and then someone sent us the very sum we needed."

Steve and Marlene looked at one another. "Last Monday....," Steve said. "Do you mind telling us how much you needed?"

When Tony revealed the amount, Marlene exploded.

"I knew it!" she said, turning to her husband. "We've been disobedient. God put you on our hearts, and last Sunday I was so convicted you needed three thousand dollars I almost brought the check to church. But when we saw you, and you seemed so...so *fine*, well, we just figured we must have gotten something wrong."

Marlene fumbled in her purse. "Here," she said looking at Steve for confirmation. "We have to give you this." She handed Rae a check.

"But we don't need it anymore!" Rae protested.

"That doesn't matter. I'm overwhelmed by our insensitivity to God. We need to obey Him now—I'm just sorry we didn't do it sooner!"

Rae looked down at the check in her hands. The tears stung her eyes as she read the amount it represented: three thousand dollars.

A SACK FULL OF MIRACLES

For me, working on this book has been like mining for gold. I have spent months on the telephone, chasing down leads and confirming reports. I have haunted the stacks in public and university libraries, poring through decades-old books that no one—it seemed—had cracked before me. Sometimes my labor yielded little fruit as supposedly "awesome" stories turned out to be only half-true or embellished through countless retellings.

At other times, however, I felt overwhelmed by the sheer magnitude of miracles. Stories like Rae and Tony McClellans' cropped up time and again as I saw God reaching down to bring help where it was needed. Yet the commonness of these stories did nothing to diminish their value; instead, like a miner who's caught "the fever," I found myself wanting to yell "Eureka!" with each new revelation. God, it seems to me, cannot help but be there when we need Him.

Perhaps this chapter is a bit premature. Perhaps I should have saved it for after the next chapter, which reveals how God uses miracles to answer our prayers. Prayer is, after all, the most practical means we have for bringing our specific needs before the Lord.

But, to the miner whose sack is overflowing with treasure, it doesn't much matter which nuggets fall out first. They are all beautiful, with a value beyond measure. God uses miracles to respond to our faith. He uses them to produce faith. He uses them to remove obstacles and to meet practical needs. And He uses them to answer our prayers.

Answered Prayer

We look upon prayer as a means of getting things for ourselves;
the Bible idea of prayer is that we may get to know God Himself.

—OSWALD CHAMBERS

ARY GILLIAM KNEW HE SERVED A MIRACLE-WORKING GOD, and he had heard plenty of stories that revealed the connection between miracles and prayer. Yet he had never seen or been part of a miracle himself. He wanted to, though, so he decided to ask God to show him a miracle.

Gary prayed, and he expected God to hear him. Even so, he was startled one morning when, at five o'clock, a powerful, loving voice interrupted his slumber. "My son," the voice said, "I want you to go to a small town in Georgia, just south of Jackson, and look for that Pentecostal Lutheran."

Rubbing the sleep from his eyes, Gary struggled to comprehend the message. He and his wife ran a nondenominational church camp, and they had met people from all religious backgrounds. Never had he encountered anyone who called himself a "Pentecostal Lutheran." Gary couldn't help but be a bit skeptical.

"God," he said, "if that's really You, tell me something else."

By now Gary was wide awake, and there was no mistaking the audible voice that filled his room. "You'll go to Georgia, you'll drive a green car, and you'll talk to ten men."

Instead of clearing things up, that answer only added to Gary's confusion. He didn't even own a car—much less a green one. And besides, Jackson was more than six hundred miles away. Nonetheless, Gary knew he had heard the voice of God, and he sensed that his miracle was about to happen.

A few days later the first piece of the puzzle fell into place when Gary's brother-in-law got a new car and offered Gary his old one. It was a green Chevrolet. With no real idea as to where he was headed, Gary packed his bags, kissed his wife good-bye, and headed south to Georgia.

He drove all night. The next morning, as he pulled into Jackson, Gary realized the senselessness of his position. He wanted to see a miracle, but he had no idea where to turn. He continued to pray, and driving slowly through the town, he pulled into a church parking lot, where he met one of the pastors. Gary asked him if he knew any Pentecostal Lutherans.

The man looked quizzically at Gary before answering. "I've never heard of a Pentecostal Lutheran. But if you'll come into my office, I'll make a few phone calls."

Gary followed the pastor into the church, where a number of calls failed to turn up any leads. No one, it seemed, knew anyone who could be considered a Pentecostal Lutheran. Finally, however, another pastor offered a clue. "We don't have any Pentecostals in this town," he said, "at least none that I know of. But a few years ago a couple who visited our church started some sort of home fellowship group on the outskirts of town. They might know something."

Grateful for any lead, no matter how slim, Gary drove to the couple's house. A woman answered his knock, and he introduced himself. "My name is Gary. I just drove up in a green car. Does that mean anything to you?"

The woman immediately locked her screen door, but as Gary explained his situation, she seemed to soften. "You'll want to talk to my husband," she said. "He's meeting with several men down at Bob Long's Chevrolet dealership."

Gary was beginning to feel his lack of sleep when he reached the car lot and introduced himself to a small group of men. "I'm looking for a Pentecostal Lutheran," he said. Gary had repeated the phrase so often that it rolled easily off his tongue. Even so, the men could not think of anyone who fit the unusual description.

Sensing Gary's fatigue, one of the men invited him to join his family for dinner and then spend the night in an apartment behind his house. Later that evening, during dinner, the telephone rang. It was Bob Long, the fellow who owned the car dealership. He sounded excited.

"My wife and I just realized something," he said. "My grandfather was a Lutheran minister. I was raised as a Lutheran—but now I'm a Penecostal. *I'm the guy!*"

Bob invited Gary to come to his house and meet his wife, Mary. Gary accepted and, thanking his hosts for the meal, he grabbed his jacket and his Bible. He arrived at the Longs' home, still uncertain as to why he was there. He met Mary and the Longs' two young sons. Then, not knowing what else to say, he invited the couple to pray.

Gary began a general sort of prayer, and then, before he could stop himself, he heard himself describing a litany of arguments and destructive patterns that marked the couple's marriage. Gary knew he ought to be embarrassed to speak of the intimate details in these strangers' relationship, but he felt compelled to continue.

Bob and Mary sat dumbfounded by what they heard. There was no denying that their unusual guest spoke the truth—*but how could he know such things?* Old wounds and communication problems paled beside Gary's powerful words, and Bob and Mary did not need to exchange looks to know what each was thinking:

God had sent a total stranger six hundred miles to get their attention, and His message was right on the mark.

Gary continued speaking until some time after midnight. As they soaked up his words, the change in Bob and Mary was unmistakable. Gary could tell something incredible was taking place: Bob and Mary's marriage was being healed.

The following day Gary began his drive home. It was raining, but nothing could dampen his enthusiasm. He had heard God's voice, which was miracle enough, he thought. He had gone to Georgia, driven a green car, and talked with…yes, he realized, *exactly ten men*. Even more wonderful, though, was that he had been privileged to serve as God's messenger: He had seen the Lord restore a marriage right before his eyes.

Gary slowed down to navigate his car through the rain. As he did, he heard God speak again: "I sent you there to answer that little boy's prayers." He became confused.

What, Gary wondered, did that mean? Unable to answer his own question, Gary tucked God's words away in the back of his mind. One more missing puzzle piece.

This time, Gary did not have to wait for an answer. A letter arrived from the Longs, describing how their seven-year-old son, Aaron, had stood up in church. "Mom and Dad used to fight all the time," the child had said, "and I used to get out of bed and pray. I knew my Jesus could help."

Gary read the words over again: *I knew my Jesus could help*. Little Aaron had prayed for his parents, just as Gary had asked God to show him a miracle. Gary smiled to himself. *How very like God to use one miracle to answer two different prayers.*

GLAD YOU ASKED

Stories like Gary Gilliam's show that God works miracles in answer to prayer. Of course, as Dr. Wayne Grudem notes, Christians see answers to prayer every day.

Grudem teaches at Trinity Evangelical Divinity School, and he points out that "we should not water down our definition of a miracle so much that every answer to pray is called a miracle. But when an answer to prayer is so remarkable that people involved with it are amazed and acknowledge God's power at work in an unusual way, then it seems appropriate to call it a miracle."[1]

Working according to Grudem's definition, Scripture is full of stories in which genuine miracles occur in answer to prayer: God raised a widow's dead son when the prophet Elijah asked him to, Jesus cured a deaf and mute man when the fellow's friends begged for a healing, and Peter experienced an astonishing jailbreak when the early Christians prayed.[2] Each of these instances produced a domino effect in terms of people glorifying God and coming to faith, but the miracles themselves were wrought simply because people prayed.

This scriptural link between prayer and miracles repeats itself in contemporary life—demonstrating yet again that God knows our needs and is glad when we ask Him to meet them. And, as Grudem points out, if God really does work a miracle in answer to our prayers, it is important that we "not ignore it or go to great lengths to devise possible 'natural causes' to explain away what God has in fact done."[3]

Skeptics may search for ways to paint God's hand out of the picture, but for people like Aileen Giddens, there is no use trying to mask a miracle when it happens. Aileen saw God answer her prayers in an amazing way, and like others who have experienced the supernatural, she knows that what happened was, in fact, a miracle.

ONLY A MIRACLE

For Aileen Giddens, life moved too fast for her thoughts to keep pace. Her wedding was less than five months away, and it seemed she had a thousand things to do. She and Dave had settled on a date, but there were dresses to be made, flowers to order, china patterns to choose, and photographers to interview. Sitting in her doctor's office, she was almost glad she had nothing to do but wait.

Within moments, however, flowers and china patterns seemed millions of miles away. Aileen's doctor delivered the devastating news: A cyst the size of a grapefruit was on one of her ovaries. Surgery to remove the ovary would be scheduled immediately.

Aileen explained the situation to Dave, uncertain as to how he would respond. He was not given to overt displays of emotion or expression, yet the strength of his quiet answer amazed her. "I will always be with you," he said, "and together, we need to look to God."

Almost before she knew what was happening, Aileen found herself on the operating table, where—she later learned—the doctors discovered her other ovary was coated with endometriosis. They had no choice but to remove part of that ovary as well as the other, leaving only a small piece—and an even smaller chance that Aileen would ever be able to have children.

As their wedding approached, Aileen took Dave's counsel to heart. God, she knew, was in control—both of her body and of their future.

The doctors had said that Aileen's best chance of getting pregnant was early in their marriage because the endometriosis was apt to grow back. Months passed, and Dave and Aileen celebrated their first anniversary. They were more in love with each other than ever. Still, they longed for a baby.

Aileen made regular visits to her doctor, who detected no accumulation of endometriosis. Thus, when her doctor discovered a second cyst, the news came as a devastating blow. The growth was as big as a lemon and had lodged itself around Aileen's single remaining ovary. Aileen realized the chance of her ever having children—a long shot until now—had been eliminated. Her only hope was a miracle.

Aileen called virtually everyone she knew, asking her friends to pray and to pass the word to other believers. They created a far-reaching chain of prayer, linked with people who were willing to ask and trust God for the answer. Aileen leaned heavily on Dave, whose confidence in God's ability to heal provided the emotional and spiritual boost she needed as her second operation drew near.

Aileen's faith was strong, but she could not have predicted what happened next: *When the doctors tried to remove the cyst, they could not find it.* It had been a solid mass—and yet it had simply disappeared. Could it be that their interpretation of the ultrasound had been wrong, that the cyst was only a fluid-filled lump that had dissolved of its own accord?

Aileen's doctor did not think so. Moreover, he marveled at what he saw when he cleared out the endometriosis that had regrown in Aileen's system: Her remaining ovary, small as it was, was in perfect working condition.

There could be only one explanation. "Aileen," the doctor said, "I think we can call this a miracle."

But the miracle didn't end there. Two years later Aileen learned she was pregnant. She gave birth to a healthy baby girl, and today little Melissa is looking forward to her second birthday. She'll have a party and a cake, of course—but as a testimony to God's goodness, she'll also have a new baby brother or sister who can watch her blow out the candles.

ANOTHER MIRACLE BABY

Aileen's story might strike a strong chord with Lara Woods. Like Aileen, Lara looked forward to motherhood, and her job as a pediatric nurse only strengthened her love for children. Working in the pediatric intensive care unit at Vanderbilt hospital—where her husband, Joe, was a plastic surgery fellow—Lara saw infants and children struggle against disease, deformation, and even death. Despite the tragedy she often faced, Lara loved her profession. Nothing, she thought, could be better than helping a child triumph over sickness and despair.

When Lara learned she was pregnant, she and Joe could scarcely contain their joy. They heard the baby's heartbeat, and their anticipation grew. They could hardly wait for the ultrasound; a routine examination, it would allow them to "see" their eighteen-week-old baby as he or she kicked and moved in Lara's uterus.

The day finally came, and as the technician manipulated the ultrasound equipment, Joe and Lara watched in fascination. They had seen ultrasound pictures before, but these images were special. They were watching their very own child—and already they were in love.

"Oh, my gosh," the technician said, interrupting the couple's reverie. "Wait a minute...um, excuse me."

With no more explanation, the technician left the room. Time dragged on, and Lara and Joe began to wonder. Was this standard procedure? Vanderbilt was a teaching hospital—and therefore, notoriously slow—but surely they could not be expected to wait much longer. Finally the door opened, and a radiologist introduced himself.

The radiologist read the ultrasound and without elaboration said, "You need to see your doctor right now."

Numb and confused, Lara and Joe made their way to the obstetrician's office. "What's going on?" Lara pleaded to Joe. He did not know; never before had either of them experienced such a sense of frustration. *Was this how all patients felt, they wondered—like victims?*

Lara's doctor was gentle and kind, yet nothing could take the sting out of his words. "There is a problem with your baby," he said.

With that, Lara's pent-up emotions broke loose, and she began to sob. Dimly, she heard the doctor explain the situation. A right choroid plexus cyst about half the size of a dime had developed in the baby's brain. As she struggled to comprehend what that meant, Lara realized the doctor was still speaking.

"This problem is extremely rare," he said. "In fact, I've never actually seen this before now. There are people at this hospital who will advise you to abort the pregnancy, but I believe there is a chance—however remote—that things may be all right. I'd advise you, though, not to read the literature on this condition. It will only discourage you."

Lara and Joe thanked the physician—and made a beeline for the university's medical library. Joe located the appropriate manual and began leafing through the pages. *Right choroid plexus, right choroid plexus*...There it was. Together, the couple read the grim report.

The cyst was associated with a chromosomal abnormality that was not, the manual said, compatible with life. The anomalies associated with the syndrome included neurological and cardiac defects, and babies born with the condition could only be expected to live for hours or, in some cases, a few days.

Lara let the words sink in. She refused to consider an abortion—but how, she wondered, could she ever handle this pregnancy? In the past few weeks she had seen two nurses on her unit give birth to deformed babies, and another baby was stillborn. *How could she make it through something like that?*

Lara spent the weekend in bed while Joe threw himself into his work. Fearful that friends or family might offer advice she did not want to hear, Lara kept her secret to herself, refusing to answer the telephone or share her concerns with anyone. Her baby had formed abnormally, and now all Lara wanted was to be left alone—alone with her helpless, precious, unborn child.

Monday evening came, and with it the Woodses' regular small-group Bible study. They had only known the people in the group for a few months, but already Lara and Joe counted them among their closest friends. Lara resolved to keep her chin up and go to the meeting.

But when she walked through the door, her resolve melted, and she burst into tears. "What is it?" asked her friends. "Lara, what's wrong?"

Lara looked at Joe for support. "Our baby is not normal," she said. "There's a cyst on its brain."

Immediately the group started to pray. Forming a circle about Lara, they put their hands on her head, her shoulders, and her stomach. One after the other they prayed, their words punctuated by muffled sobs as some in the group began to cry softly.

The prayer ended, leaving Lara filled with a sense of relief. For the first time since she had learned of the problem four days ago, she felt peace. Her burden had lifted, and she knew that God was with her and that He would walk her through whatever trials the future held.

A follow-up ultrasound was scheduled for Lara's thirtieth week of pregnancy, at which time the doctors expected to be able to learn more about the size and nature of the problem. In the interim, Lara met with another obstetrician, who did not mask her feelings. "You realize that you are already past the time when you can safely end this pregnancy," she said. "You need to seriously consider having an abortion—my duty as an obstetrician is to tell you that you need to do it *now*."

Lara thanked the woman for her professional advice and ended the discussion. She knew she could not abort her baby. Moreover, she could not escape the strange sensation that, even as she carried her unborn child, God was somehow carrying her, bearing her along in His arms.

When the follow-up ultrasound appointment arrived, Joe excused himself from surgery and joined Lara in the technician's office. The technician was not the same fellow who had discovered the cyst, but he had read the charts and his look was not encouraging. Lara held her breath as she waited for his report. Had the cyst grown? Was it worse than she and Joe anticipated?

The technician moved his instruments and began muttering to himself. "I do not believe this," he said over and over again.

Lara's heart was in her throat and she began to weep. "What?" she demanded. "Is it worse? *Is the baby dead?*"

"No," the technician replied. "The cyst is not there. I mean, I can't find it. I need someone else to come and look."

The radiologist was summoned, and as he reviewed the pictures he shook his head. "This is very unusual," he said. "These cysts rarely go away."

The radiologist maintained his composure, but the technician could not hold back. "This is wonderful!" he exclaimed, and then he began to cry. "I mean, this is so *weird!*"

"Well, this baby has been prayed for," Lara said, through her own grateful tears. She turned to Joe, who had a look of wonder on his face. After four years of medical school and six years in residency, he understood something that none of his schooling had taught him: God is greater than anything science and medicine have to offer. His power, unlike a surgeon's, knows no limits.

Ten weeks later Lara gave birth to a baby girl named Emily. It was the middle of the night, and the pediatrician who examined Emily had tears in his eyes. "You have a perfectly normal baby girl," he said. "I heard about this baby from a friend who is in your small group, and I have been praying for you for the past ten weeks. This is truly a miracle baby."

HUNGRY FOR SIGNS

Stories like the Woodses' make me wonder why anyone who understands God's power, grace, and responsiveness would be adverse to praying for miracles. Yet I can think of countless examples of times when people who needed help either refused or forgot to pray. King Asa, for instance, is someone whose behavior has always puzzled me.

Asa ruled in ancient Judah almost one thousand years before the time of Christ. History remembers him as a good king who obeyed the Lord. He recognized God's power and called on it during battle, with great success. After reigning for thirty-nine years, however, Asa contracted some sort of foot disease. It was apparently quite serious, yet he chose not to call on the Lord for help. Instead, he turned to his physicians. Within two years, he was dead.[4]

Asa had a personal history of answers from God, and he must have heard the miracle stories that peppered Israel's history. God had a track record of working miracles in answer to the prayers of His people; what would have happened if Asa had asked God to heal his feet? More importantly, why did he fail to pray for a miracle?

In a cover story on miracles, Time magazine described the verification process imposed by the Catholic church before a miracle can be considered a supernatural and genuine answer to prayer. Roger Pilon, head of the International Medical Committee that scrutinizes the miracles reported at the shrine of Lourdes, says that as medical science and psychology uncover rational explanations for more cures, it is getting harder and harder to label an event a miracle. This trend is one he regrets, suggesting that the church gives more importance to cases that include divine intervention—even if that is not the only explanation for the cure. "Ordinary Christians want to see the action of God," Pilon says. "People are hungry for signs."[5]

If so, then perhaps more people should pray.

CHAPTER 8

God's Stamp of Approval

Lord, make me an instrument of Thy peace. Where there is hatred, let me sow love;
where there is injury, pardon; where there is doubt, faith; where there is despair, hope;
where there is sadness, joy; where there is darkness, light.

—ST. FRANCIS OF ASSISI

ORREST BEISER WAS JUST NINETEEN YEARS OLD when he signed up for a summer missions outreach to Sri Lanka. His job, along with five other college students, was to preach at impromptu crusades in various cities. Bus depots, open-air markets, and city squares became makeshift pulpits as the young missionaries erected hastily built platforms and began to share their message. The fact that there were no microphones or stage lights mattered little to Forrest; if anything, the humble props served to enhance his sense of being in touch with the masses of humanity that thronged past his platform each day.

After three weeks of preaching every day until his throat felt hoarse, Forrest had not lost any of his enthusiasm. He looked forward to discussing ministry results with others on the team. When the group convened, however, Forrest's elation turned to doubt as, one after the other, the college students recounted their experiences. Everyone, it seemed, had seen incredible miracles take place when they ministered. Everyone, that is, except Forrest.

"You should be seeing some things happen," suggested the team leader gently.

Forrest agreed—yet he had no idea how to "make" a miracle. Could it be he was not cut out for this type of ministry? Did his message lack the power and conviction of his teammates' preaching? Was he—or his presentation of the gospel—not up to God's standards?

A BASIS FOR BELIEF

Forrest's desire to see miracles happen was not born of curiosity or a need for flashy showmanship. Instead, he understood one of the primary purposes for miracles: God uses miracles to authenticate the message of the gospel. Forrest wanted God's stamp of approval on the message he preached.

The Bible talks about signs, wonders, and mighty works in conjunction with miracles. *Signs* point to God's presence and confirm His message. *Wonders* inspire awe and amazement in those who see them. And *mighty works* reveal God's power and His ability to work miracles.

Over and over again we see signs, wonders, and mighty works being used to validate God's message. After Christ's resurrection, for example, the disciples "went out and preached everywhere, the Lord working with them and confirming the word through the accompanying signs."[1] Likewise, Paul and Barnabas presented the gospel with God "bearing witness to the word of His grace, granting signs and wonders to be done by their hands."[2]

In validating the gospel in such an extraordinarily powerful and unusual manner, signs and wonders also serve to draw people to God. Jesus recognized this relationship and said, "Believe Me that I am in the Father and the Father in Me, or else believe Me for the sake of the works themselves."[3] In other words, if people could not believe what Christ said about Himself, they were welcome to anchor their faith in the evidence of His miracles. Christ knew that actions, for some people, really do speak louder than words.

Certainly this principle was in evidence in Peter's ministry. When he happened upon a man who had been paralyzed and bedridden for eight years, Peter did not hesitate to point the man toward Christ. "Jesus the Christ heals you," he said. "Arise and make your bed." The man immediately stood to his feet—and, according to Luke's careful record, *all* the townspeople saw him and turned to the Lord.[4]

News of what had happened to the paralytic traveled fast, and when a beloved disciple named Tabitha died in a neighboring town, the other disciples immediately summoned Peter. He arrived to find Tabitha's room filled with mourning widows. They clustered around him, crying. Hardly daring to hope for a miracle, the women focused their attention on the lovely robes and other garments Tabitha had made in her life of serving others. Truly, they agreed, she had been a remarkable woman.

Peter sent the mourners out of the room. Alone with the dead woman, he got down on his knees and prayed. He turned toward her and said simply, "Tabitha, arise." Tabitha opened her eyes, saw Peter, and sat up. Taking her by the hand, Peter presented her to the small crowd waiting outside the room. Not surprisingly, word of this dramatic resurrection spread like wildfire. Again, as with the miraculous healing of the paralytic, many people believed in the Lord.[5]

Nineteen-year-old Forrest Beiser had studied the Bible, and he was no stranger to stories like these. He recognized the power of miracles to validate the gospel message and draw people to Christ. What's more, he knew God used miracles to confirm the authority of His servants. Forrest wanted to see miracles in his ministry because he wanted the assurance that he—like his teammates—was a messenger chosen by God.

UNDENIABLE AUTHORITY

Forrest would have understood Nicodemus's perspective when, two thousand years ago, the Pharisee paid a visit to Jesus, presumably "off the record" since he came at night, under the cover of darkness. The Pharisees were not known for their support of Christ; on the contrary, they tried to entrap Him at every turn. Yet Nicodemus could not deny Christ's authority, and unable to contain his curiosity, he blurted out his feelings: "Rabbi," he said, "we know that You are a teacher come from God; for no one can do these signs that You do unless God is with him."[6]

As a Pharisee, Nicodemus had spent his life studying the law and the prophets. He must have known about Moses and his commission to lead God's people out of Egypt. "Who am *I* to do that job?" Moses had protested. "What if the people do not believe me when I tell them that this whole thing was Your idea, God?"

The Lord had a ready answer. "What is that in your hand?"

"A rod," Moses replied.

"Cast it on the ground."

When Moses did so, his rod turned into a snake. Then, as if that weren't enough, God told him to pick up the creature. When Moses touched the serpent's tail, it became a staff again in his hand. This, said the Lord, is so "that they may believe that the LORD God of their fathers,... has appeared to you."

Then, as though for good measure, God told Moses to place his hand inside his cloak. When he took it out, it was leprous—until he put it back in again. But even after the snake and the leprous hand, God knew, there might yet be some skeptics in the crowd. "If they do not believe even these two signs, or listen to your voice," God said, "take some water from the Nile and pour it on the dry ground. It will turn into blood."[7]

Talk about miracles! There was nothing subtle or ordinary about these signs, yet Moses did not exploit them or use them to draw attention to himself. Instead, Scripture tells us, Moses was the most humble man on the face of the earth.[8] He never saw miracles as a way to elevate himself; rather, he continually pointed people toward the power and authority of God.

In this display of humility, Moses illustrated a critical point about the role of miracles. They are never meant to exalt or glorify the messenger; rather, they validate the message itself as being sent from God. And even as signs and wonders confirmed Moses' authority to lead the Israelites out of Egypt, his was clearly a *delegated* commission. Nowhere in Scripture—from Moses through the apostles in the early church—do miracles underscore the power and authority of any person except Jesus Christ.

A Man Marked by God

In many respects, Moses reminds me of a thirteenth-century figure, Saint Francis of Assisi. Committed to a life of self-denial, Saint Francis urged his brothers in the faith to imitate Christ's humility, obedience, and service. In his book *The Medieval World*, Friedrich Heer notes how the life of Saint Francis stood as a rebuke to the prevailing cultural forces of his day: He preached a doctrine of Christian service to the politically powerful papacy, and he became a symbol of peacemaking before the bloodletting crusaders. And to those who put Christianity down as merely a bunch of lofty ideals, Saint Francis brought home the reality of the passion and crucifixion of Jesus.[9]

It was out of this desire to identify with Christ's passion and suffering that the most remarkable miracle in Saint Francis's life occurred. Early one morning, before dawn, Francis knelt in prayer. "Oh Lord," he pleaded, "I beg of You two graces before I die—to experience in myself all possible fullness the pains of

Your cruel Passion, and to feel for You the same love that made You sacrifice Yourself for us."[10]

As Francis continued to pray, his heart burned with love and pity. "Suddenly appeared to him a seraph with six wings, bearing enfolded in them a very beautiful image of a crucified man, his hands and feet outflung as on a cross, with features clearly resembling those of the Lord Jesus."

Francis understood that this vision revealed that he was to be "utterly transformed into the likeness of the crucified Christ, not by the torture of his body but by the love inflaming his soul."[11] An unearthly light appeared, and when the vision faded, Francis found himself marked with the wounds of Christ—the stigmata. His hands and feet appeared as though pierced with nails. Real, round black nailheads stood out on his palms and feet, with bent points protruding out on the back of his hands and the soles of his feet. Moreover, Francis bore a lance wound in his side from which blood frequently flowed—so much so that it soaked his tunic.[12]

Although Francis sought to keep his wounds bandaged and hidden in the sleeves of his habit, they never went away. A number of people saw the marks—including Pope Alexander IV—and several gave sworn testimony to their existence.

Francis's stigmatization was regarded as something unique and unprecedented. History has since seen several stigmatics come forward in imitation of the miracle, including a number of twentieth-century cases that have survived medical scrutiny and defied rational explanation. What, actually, were the stigmata?

One scholar describes the stigmata as "the exterior signs of the interior wound of love."[13] In Francis's case, these exterior signs were commonly taken to be the convincing evidence of his saintliness, proof of his absolute identification with Christ. They were, as one writer put it, "God's imprimatur."[14]

This phrase—*God's imprimatur*—sums up both the reason behind and the significance of Saint Francis's stigmata. His wounds served as God's "official seal," given in response to Saint Francis's demonstration of Christlikeness in his passion and love. The seal conveyed a message: Saint Francis was a man marked by the Lord.

SURPRISED BY GOD

Before he received the stigmata, Saint Francis apparently sensed via divine revelation that something unusual—and in fact, marvelous—was about to happen. He said as much to one of his companions, and as Francis sought clarification of this vision, he learned that he was to imitate Christ in all the afflictions and pains of His passion. Instead of being frightened by the prospect, Francis rejoiced at the privilege.[15] Perhaps the fact that he had seen it coming prepared him for God's intervention.

Forrest Beiser, on the other hand, could not have predicted what would happen as he continued to preach and minister in Sri Lanka. He did not expect a miracle; he only hoped God would perform one.

It was just after the group meeting—the one where Forrest realized he had the dubious distinction of being the only missionary in his program who had not personally witnessed or experienced miracles. Forrest and his interpreter, Irvin, found a new street, erected their platform, and began to preach.

By midafternoon Forrest guessed that probably a thousand people had heard the gospel, or at least part of it. It was hard to tell who was really listening as the crowds ebbed and flowed through the street. His voice was almost gone when he announced that he would begin to pray for people.

A line formed immediately. Accustomed to spending hours talking with and praying for the people who waited patiently in the street, Forrest and Irvin started to pray. After ministering to forty or fifty people, Forrest still had not seen anything unusual or miraculous, but he sensed that his efforts were not in vain. God, he figured, heard and answered prayers—with or without miracles.

As he prayed, Forrest became aware of a blind man making his way toward the front of the line. Led by a girl of about seven, the man moved slowly until he stood directly in front of Forrest. His eyes were white, almost like they did not exist at all. Filled with compassion, Forrest asked the Lord to have mercy on the man and heal his eyesight.

When Forrest finished praying, the blind man—like the masses who had gone before him—eased toward the edge of the platform. Obviously, he had not been healed. Suddenly, though, Irvin's voice rang out. "Come back!" he commanded. "We need to pray again."

Before Forrest realized what was happening, he heard his own voice rise above Irvin's: "The Lord is going to heal this man!"

What did I just say? Forrest could not believe his ears—but had no time for second thoughts. Even without a microphone, his voice had carried through the street, and a throng of people pushed toward the platform. "Did you hear?" they said, jostling one another. "A miracle is going to happen. Move over—hey, down in front! I want to see!"

Forrest ignored the crush of the crowd and began to pray. "Jesus, I don't know what to do," he said, "but if You heal this man, those people watching right now are going to know You."

Instinctively he put his thumbs on the blind man's eyes. With his own eyes closed, Forrest continued to pray. Moments later, he looked up—and beheld two of the brightest, bluest eyes he had ever seen! There he was, eye to eye with a man who—just seconds earlier—had been without any real eyes at all. Overcome by his own amazement, Forrest fainted.

When he woke up, he found himself in bed. The full impact of what had happened came rushing back. How could such a miracle have occurred? Forrest asked himself. *I'm only nineteen years old—and God used me!* It was almost too wonderful to be true.

As Forrest replayed the scene in his mind, Irvin filled him in on what had happened. The man had, in fact, received his eyesight, leaving the crowd in absolute awe. Everyone, it seemed, was talking about the miracle.

Sure enough, when Forrest and Irvin resumed their ministry the following day, the crowd had swelled to a multitude. This time, however, people did not just hurry by as they went about their business. Instead, many came just to listen—hoping to witness another demonstration of the missionaries' loving and powerful God. They wanted to know more about Jesus.

Today Forrest pastors a church in San Francisco. He has seen other miracles over the years, but few—if any—are so memorable as the blind man's healing. When God intervened that day, it changed more than the blind man's life. The miracle was God's megaphone—both for an unbelieving crowd that thronged the city streets and for a young missionary, longing for God's stamp of approval.

Whether they build faith, overcome obstacles to ministry and service, meet practical needs, answer prayers, or validate the gospel message, miracles point toward God and draw people to Him. Once we approach the Almighty, though, who are we going to find?

The chapters in the next section of this book offer at least a partial response to this question. God works miracles—and when He does, He offers a window on His nature. Whether we peer through the glass or go so far as to climb over the sill, we will discover the maker of miracles: the awesome, loving, sovereign God.

PART THREE

The Miracle Maker

That's Awesome!

[God] performs wonders that cannot be fathomed,
miracles that cannot be counted.

—JOB 9:10 NIV

HERYL PREWITT RELAXED IN THE FAMILIAR SURROUNDINGS of her doctor's office. Six years earlier her left leg had been crushed in a tragic car accident that put her in a body cast for three months. Just eleven years old at the time, she had sustained multiple fractures and damage to her bones, and her doctors had said she would never walk again.

Cheryl had defied their predictions. Thanks to her faith in God, her leg mended and she learned to walk again. Now, as a seventeen-year-old anticipating her senior year of high school, Cheryl hardly noticed the slight limp that served as the only visible reminder of her injuries. Her left leg was two inches shorter than the right one, but she was in good health. Her medical checkups were routine, and she regarded her doctor as an old friend.

She was not prepared for his report this time. "There's a potential problem with your leg," the doctor said, his gentle tone doing little to mask his concern.

"Problem?" Cheryl repeated. "What kind of problem?"

"Well, it's nothing to worry about now, but because of the way your leg mended, your hips are out of line, and you may never be able to have children."

It was hard to fathom the impact of the doctor's words. Motherhood had always been a distant expectation, not an immediate goal. Suddenly, though, her desire to have children was painfully real. Wasn't there something the doctors could do? Some operation that could change her fate?

Unfortunately, the only way to straighten Cheryl's hips was to make her left leg grow—something the doctors admittedly could not do.

At home, Cheryl began to read her Bible, particularly the accounts of miracles detailed in the Gospels and in Acts. It wasn't long before she began to believe God could heal her—specifically, He could lengthen her left leg. When she learned of a healing service to be held in a nearby city, she made up her mind to go.

As the day of the service approached, Cheryl grew increasingly confident that her healing was about to take place. Nevertheless, on the night before the big event, she could not sleep. It was not just nerves or excitement; Cheryl sensed that something more significant was afoot. She decided to read her Bible.

Turning to John, her favorite Gospel, Cheryl began to read. Suddenly, the words seemed to jump off the page: *"I have told you before it comes, that when it does come to pass, you may believe."*[1] Cheryl knew the Lord was sending her a message. He wanted her to know in advance that her healing would take place—specifically to serve as a witness to His reality, glory, and power. She couldn't wait to tell her friends.

At school the following day, Cheryl made a point of sharing her anticipation with about fifteen other teenagers. Until then, some of them had not known about her earlier accident or its devastating consequences. Now, as Cheryl explained her limp, she met with sympathy and surprise.

"You poor thing!" one girl cried.

"Oh, no," Cheryl countered. "Don't feel sorry for me. The only reason I'm telling you all this is that I want you to notice my legs. Tomorrow they are going to be the same length!"

The high schoolers were skeptical, but they liked Cheryl too much to poke fun at her faith. "I'll believe it when I see it," said one of her classmates, voicing the unspoken sentiments of the group.

That night, as Cheryl found a seat in the service, she could hardly contain her excitement. She watched the crowd eagerly. But when her turn came for prayer, she turned her attention to the minister, who told her to focus on Jesus.

As the minister began to pray, Cheryl felt a warm sensation envelop her body. Overwhelmed by God's power and compassion, she lost track of time as she experienced wave after wave of God's love. She closed her eyes and sank to the floor.

When she opened her eyes, the sight that greeted her took her breath away. There, extended straight forward from her body, were two perfectly matched legs. *Cheryl had experienced a miracle!* After six years, her legs were normal and her limp was gone!

The next day Cheryl told her friends what had happened and showed them her legs as proof of the miracle. Even as she recounted her experience, though, Cheryl realized her new leg was only part of God's gift. She was glad for her healing, but more than that, she was grateful to God for demonstrating His power in a way that revealed His love and His desire to become personally involved in her life.

Cheryl has never lost her awareness of God's awesome power—or the purposes for which He uses it. Crowned Miss America in 1980, she found a broad audience for her testimony. She still talks about her dramatic healing, and when she does, she is careful to point to the meaning in the miracle: God is powerful and real, and He wants nothing more than to share His boundless love with His children.

THE WITNESS OF WONDER

The healing of Cheryl's leg is remarkable. However, for those who recognize God's power and ability, it makes perfect sense that the One who created the human body in the first place would know how to repair any defects that might occur. And when you think about it, legs grow all the time as babies become children who become teenagers and then adults. In Cheryl's case, the growth was simply an immediate accomplishment—and therein lies the awesomeness of the miracle.

When I began working on this book, one of the things I wanted to find was a good definition of a miracle. I discovered several interesting possibilities, one of the most prevalent being the idea that a miracle is, quite simply, a direct intervention of God in the affairs of men. While that definition seemed essentially true, it did not, I thought, accurately reflect the special, extraordinary nature of miracles. The Bible says rain and snow come down from heaven— meaning they are examples of divine intervention in our lives.[2] Yet I have never thought of a summer shower as a miracle, except in the same way that Augustine considered all of God's creation as part of the "miracle of miracles, the world itself."[3]

Miracles are more than just the times when God takes an active role in our lives. We must acknowledge His intervention, of course—but to me, a proper miracle must also contain an element of awe. I like Dr. Wayne Grudem's definition: "A miracle," he wrote, "is a less common kind of God's activity in which he arouses people's awe and wonder and bears witness to himself."[4]

In bearing witness to God, miracles reveal His nature, including His power, His compassion, and His sovereignty. There are obviously additional aspects to God's character; the chapters in this section, however, deal specifically with how miracles illuminate these three elements.

The stories in this chapter testify to God's awesome power. They are, frankly, incredible—so much so that skeptics who thrive on logical explanations may want to dismiss the entire chapter as a pack of fantasies. Such a reaction is hardly unprecedented; ever since the time of Christ, people have been trying to "explain away" His more amazing miracles. His healings, they say, simply cured ailments that were psychosomatic to begin with while His resurrection was merely a revival from a deep coma.[5]

I believe the stories in this chapter, even as I accept the authenticity of the miracles in the Bible—however far-fetched they may appear. The New Testament teaches that miracles draw a crowd, capturing the attention—and often the hearts—of those who witness and experience them.[6] To me, it only makes sense that God, who wants to know us intimately, would use all the means at His disposal—including His awesome power—to make Himself known and get us to respond to Him.

POWER OVER NATURE, BODY, AND SOUL

Herbert Lockyer, in the introduction to his study on miracles, maintains that Christ's miracles prove beyond doubt that He had supreme command over nature and also over the soul and body of man.[7] Christ could walk on water, turn water into wine, and even raise the dead.

This power over nature, body, and soul manifests itself today in a number of ways, including the supernatural gifts the Lord bestows on people. Padre Pio was a Franciscan priest who became the subject of international curiosity and admiration in the years following World War I. The miracles that marked the friar's life included the stigmata, the gift of prophecy, and the manifestation of a perfumed odor that often accompanied or signaled his presence. Perhaps the most awe inspiring, though, was Padre Pio's gift of *bilocation*.

Bilocation is the gift of being present in two different places at the same time.

All of Padre Pio's biographers reference this unusual phenomenon, noting that, as one author put it, "the weight of acceptable evidence seems to substantiate" the miracle.[8] Stories are told of people observing Padre Pio praying at the tomb of Pope Pius XI and, on another occasion, at the beatification of Therese de Lisieux in Saint Peter's, Rome. In both cases, the humble priest was known to be following his daily routine at his monastery in Italy.[9]

Other miraculous testimonies point to more of a *translation*, or *transport*, than to bilocation. In these instances, Padre Pio's presence was not noted at the friary while he was ministering elsewhere; instead, the miracle lies in his sudden appearing during times of need. One such story concerns a Mr. Magurno who, the doctors said, had only a few hours to live.

Magurno's wife, Ersilia, telegraphed Padre Pio, asking for his help, and received an immediate answer. She knew the priest was praying for her husband—yet Magurno grew closer and closer to death. Ersilia sent a second telegram.

It was not long before Magurno fell fast asleep. To Ersilia's joy, he seemed to be resting peacefully, although he had a slight fever. Early the next morning, she inquired as to how he was feeling.

"I am feeling splendid," he replied. "Padre Pio has just left me."

Ersilia was incredulous. "Are you serious?" she asked. "What did he say?"

"First he examined my heart," Magurno explained, "and said, 'This temperature will pass, and tomorrow you will be all right. After four days you will leave your bed.' Then he looked around, examined the medicines, read the charts, and remained in the room for the rest of the night."

Five months later, the story goes, Mr. and Mrs. Magurno drove to Padre Pio's town to meet and personally thank him for his prayers. Magurno immediately recognized the priest—who, in turn, greeted him warmly. "What a deal of trouble that heart of yours gave you!" the friar said.[10]

Accounts like this one would seem far-fetched to me were it not for three things. First, in accepting the veracity of the miracles in the Bible, it is not difficult for me to make the mental leap from believing that Christ could *transform* one boy's lunch into a spread that fed five thousand people to accepting the fact that he could *transport* a modern-day friar.

Next, people who have spent substantially more time than I have investigating Padre Pio have confirmed his miracles. If there were a crack in the stories, surely it would have been discovered by now.

Finally, I believe the stories about Padre Pio because I personally know someone else who was supernaturally transported by the Lord. Dallas Plemmons is not as well known as Padre Pio but, to me, his life is no less amazing.

AGAINST IMPOSSIBLE ODDS

Toward the end of the Korean War, Dallas Plemmons was captured by Chinese Communists after a battle near the Yalu River, which separates communist North Korea from Manchuria and Siberia. Most of Dallas's company had died in the fight, and he was thrown in with a group of prisoners, many of whom were wounded. For three days the American soldiers were forced to march northward without food or water. When a prisoner was too weak to move, the Communists simply shot or bayoneted him and marched on.

The group crossed the Yalu into Manchuria, which is part of communist China. Moving at night to avoid detection by American planes, the Chinese soldiers herded their prisoners along a narrow path that wandered around a steep mountain. Suddenly, a young fellow walking directly in front of Dallas stumbled and fell. He was too weak to get up, so Dallas grabbed him and jerked him to his feet. After a few more steps, the boy fell again.

Once more, Dallas hoisted the fellow up, knowing another stumble would not escape the wrath of their captors. Sure enough, a Chinese guard moved in to watch, and when the young soldier's legs buckled a third time, the guard swung his rifle at the boy's head.

Without thinking, Dallas kicked the guard with all the force he could muster, then dove over the side of the mountain. The drop was almost straight down, just about the length of a football field. Dallas tumbled head over heels, unwilling to grab at the scrub bushes and rocks for fear of being hit by the Chinese, who were spending their ammunition on Dallas and all the other men who had desperately followed his lead.

Dallas fell into a ravine and finally hit the bottom. One by one, the other prisoners fell on top of him, killed by the fall and the hail of bullets. After what seemed like an eternity, Dallas crept out, soaking wet with the blood of his companions. It was twenty degrees below zero, and he was all alone.

"Lord," Dallas cried, "what am I to do? I can't even think!"

"Son," came the audible reply, "when did I leave you?"

Dallas began to walk through the snow with no idea which way to go and no real plan for survival. Eating whatever he could find, he made his way through the country until finally he spotted the Yalu River spread out below him. Dallas was high on a mountain, and everywhere he looked, he could see Chinese troops stationed all along the riverbank.

Dallas knew he had to get across that river. He also knew there were only two roads and both would be swarming with enemy troops. A further complication—one that Dallas did not want to even think about yet—was the jagged mountain range that stood, on the far side of the river, between the Yalu and the American lines.

As Dallas contemplated the hopelessness of his plight, he suddenly found himself across both the river and the mountain range. *How did it happen?* Could he have possibly gone into some sort of trance and staggered his way through the perilous terrain? Even as he asked the question, Dallas knew the answer: No. He would certainly have been captured or shot. Had he made such a journey successfully, it would have been a miracle—even more than his unexplainable and instantaneous transport.

Making his way toward the American lines, Dallas heard the crack of an American rifle. Stung by the bullet, he saw an American soldier and began yelling. His English, however, meant little; there were Russian agents and plenty of Chinese who knew the language. And besides, Dallas was wearing an old Chinese uniform. For all the Americans could tell, he was the enemy.

"Aw, come on now," Dallas called, "you never heard a Chinaman speak with a North Carolina accent!"

That did it. The American soldiers allowed Dallas to walk into their camp. Amazingly, he had returned to his old regiment—men he had known and told about his faith in the Lord for months before he was captured.

"My Lord, man, you're not even human!" said his sergeant upon seeing Dallas's ragged, half-dead condition.

"Yes, I am just as human as anybody else," Dallas replied. "I just serve a great big God."

"Boy, I believe it. I sure believe it."

Dallas's story was investigated by American intelligence officers, who could not explain how he had covered so much ground in so little time. Obviously, though, he had been in Manchuria; his knowledge of places and landmarks proved he had indeed been captured and taken into China. The officers were puzzled, but to Dallas, the experience only cemented his belief in an awesome, miracle-working Lord. And even better, it stood as a witness to the men in his regiment, who could not deny the saving power of God.[11]

Dallas's story, like Cheryl's healing and the miracles associated with Padre Pio, testifies to the fact that, as Grudem said, miracles arouse people's awe and wonder. But, as with all miracles, God did not intervene in these people's lives simply to leave us amazed. Instead, each of the miracles had a purpose. The healing of Cheryl's leg came in response to her faith and in answer to her prayers. Padre Pio's healing ministry met practical needs while validating the gospel he preached. And Dallas saw God overcome more than one incredible obstacle that stood between a helpless young soldier and freedom.

Each of these miracles also had an even bigger impact as those who witnessed or heard about the miracles recognized God as the source of the power.

God wants to know us and to make Himself known. Sometimes He tips His hand with fireworks and a big brass band, as when He displays His awe-inspiring might. At other times, though, His nearness is soft and gentle, full of compassion. In the next chapter we will focus on this merciful aspect of God's character as we see how miracles reveal His loving heart.

Heart-to-Heart

...But, O! th' exceeding grace
Of highest God, that loves his creatures so,
And all his works with mercy doth embrace,
That blessed angels he sends to and fro,
To serve to wicked man, to serve his wicked foe.

—EDMUND SPENSER, FROM *THE FAERIE QUEENE*

ARLENE KLEPEES WEIGHED LESS THAN TWO POUNDS when she was born prematurely and with cerebral palsy. Her doctors did not hold out high hopes for her survival; if she did make it, they cautioned Marlene's mother and father, there was no guarantee she would ever walk, talk, or even be able to see.

Two years later Marlene's parents were killed in a motorcycle accident, and she went to live with her grandparents. By the time she was five years old, Marlene still could scarcely walk or talk much at all, and as the time drew near for her to go to school, her grandmother became concerned. With no institution or special education facilities nearby, the only option was the local public school. This prospect excited Marlene, but her grandmother was less enthusiastic.

"Marlene," she said, "don't you understand that you are different? Those kids are going to tease you. This is not going to be as much fun as you think it is!"

Marlene's grandmother need not have worried. The other students were generally kind, and Marlene made some good friends. But as time passed, she could not help but notice that her grandmother had been right. She *was* different. While the other kids learned to read and write, the teacher's aide would work with Marlene in the corner to teach her how to talk. More and more Marlene sensed she did not fit in, either at school or at home, where the people she called "Mom" and "Dad" were not really her parents.

Her seizures represented yet another problem. Studying Marlene's violent convulsions, her doctors predicted that one day they would prove fatal. Marlene still could not speak very well, but she could understand other people, and hearing the doctors' prognosis, she felt confused. Her life seemed to matter so little. "God," she asked, over and over again, "why am I even alive?"

She received an answer when she was twelve years old. Several friends invited her to attend a Youth for Christ meeting one evening, and as Marlene recalls, it was an amazing experience. When the group arrived to pick her up for the meeting, four of the parents hoisted her into the back of a station wagon, not realizing she could sit up or that her body could bend. Marlene tried to protest, but no one could understand her words.

The meeting was in an old YMCA building, complete with the steepest, highest flight of stairs Marlene had ever seen. Without trying to unhook her from her walker, Marlene's friends began dragging her up the steps. *Plunk…plunk…plunk…* Never had she been dragged such a distance. Marlene began to fear that, in the teenagers' enthusiasm, they might lose their grip. "God," she inwardly cried, "don't You even care what happens to me?"

God did care. That night, when the leaders invited people to pray, Marlene asked the Lord to come into her heart. With a certainty that defied explanation, Marlene suddenly knew why she was alive. She was alive to live for God—

regardless of her physical limitations. He had become her heavenly Father. The truth hit Marlene like a sudden ray of sunshine: She was not orphaned anymore.

Marlene's faith sustained her when, three years later, she had an accident that dramatically increased her seizures and spasms. Her condition went from bad to worse as she lost control of her legs and became confined to a wheelchair. Finally a forty-seven-hour seizure landed her in the hospital, where the doctors told her grandparents that her brain was no longer functioning.

What? Marlene thought. *I'm not brain dead! I can hear them talking—I'm alive!*

Unable to utter a sound or move a muscle, Marlene cried out to God. Immediately His answer came: *I love you, and I'm going to take care of it.* Over and over again His voice reassured her, just like a father's.

The doctors admitted they could do nothing to improve Marlene's state and transferred her to the Mayo Clinic. There a team of specialists discovered that she was not, in fact, brain dead—even though she could not even lift her head and could only barely move her eyes or mouth. In time, she gave in to despair. She could do absolutely nothing for herself, and she suspected that she made life miserable for others. If this was God's idea of taking care of the situation, well, He could just go take care of somebody else!

Suddenly, in the midst of her anger and frustration, Marlene became aware of a warm, peaceful sensation flowing around her body. She knew it was God and that He was revealing His love and mercy. The walls of her room faded away, and Marlene experienced a vision. She saw herself in a small church, reclining in her wheelchair and surrounded by a knot of people who were praying. One man in particular stood out from the group; he was tall, blond, and wearing a gray pinstriped suit.

In the next image Marlene saw a girl riding a bicycle across a lush, green lawn. She concentrated on the figure and realized she was looking at herself. Then, in big black letters, a date appeared: *March 29.* March 29 was just three weeks away. Marlene knew God was going to heal her then. She struggled to communicate this to a nurse and was rewarded when the nurse made a notation on her chart: *Marlene says she is going to walk on March 29.*

As the day drew near, Marlene began to worry. She remembered the images in her vision clearly, yet she had no idea where the church was, who the people were, or how the tall blond man fit into the picture. By now it was March 28, and she could not even speak or write to share her hopes and concerns with anyone. Was God going to let her down?

Hush. Marlene sensed God's voice, and forced herself to pay attention. *In the morning have the nurse get the yellow pages,* God said, *and I will give you the name of that man who was praying for you and the name of the church.*

Marlene could hardly sleep. When the morning nurse arrived, Marlene refused to eat breakfast until the woman brought the yellow pages and flipped the phone book open for Marlene. There, in letters that seemed to glow on the page, were the words OPEN BIBLE CHURCH. Underneath the words was the pastor's name. The nurse placed the call for Marlene, who tried unsuccessfully to make herself understood. Finally the nurse grabbed the telephone. "Sir," she said, "I don't know who you are or where you are, but you had better get down here." She relayed Marlene's room number and hung up the phone.

The pastor arrived that afternoon. With the help of a nurse who could understand most of her speech, Marlene asked her visitor whether his church believed in healing.

The pastor said, "Yes, our church does believe in healing. But we have never had any." His eyes appraised Marlene's condition with uncertainty. "Do you plan on me starting with you?"

Marlene convinced the pastor to take her to his church, which turned out to be identical to the one she had seen in her vision. As several church members gathered around her to pray, Marlene wondered what she was supposed to do.

"God, I want to walk," she said, "but how? What do I do?"

As if reading her thoughts, the pastor looked at Marlene. "Do you want to stand up on faith?" he asked.

"Uhh," Marlene said, meaning "Yes." Two people grabbed her and stood her up. As they did, Marlene remembers, "Strength went from the top of my head to the very tip of my toes. I stood there and felt the floor for the very first time in my whole life! Then I took about six steps while they were hanging on to me."

The church members released their hold. Marlene started walking around the church, faster and faster. The onlookers caught her enthusiasm and joined her circuit, praising God.

"Marlene," the pastor finally broke in, "we have to stop. God gave me a sermon, and I need to preach it."

Marlene did not know how she could sit through a sermon, but she wanted to respect the pastor's wishes. He asked the congregation to open their hymnals. As she reached for the book, she realized her vision had not been healed. She could not see the words on the page. Suddenly, though, her eyes felt warm, and she sensed God telling her to take off her glasses. She did—and discovered that she could see perfectly (which was later confirmed by the Mayo Clinic eye specialists).

With this second healing, the congregation erupted. The sermon was canceled, and the jubilant crowd piled into their cars and headed off to the ice cream parlor. Marlene relished being able to hold a cone and wished the day would never end.

Finally, though, the time came to return to the hospital. Arriving in the hospital lobby, Marlene summoned a nurse from her floor. When the nurse, a man, saw her standing there without her wheelchair, he started to yell. "It's a miracle!" he shouted, grabbing Marlene and swinging her around in his arms. It was the first hug she had ever felt.

Suddenly Marlene noticed a twinkle in the nurse's eye. "Hold on," he said, retrieving her wheelchair. "Here, sit down. Let's go upstairs. I've got a plan."

The nurse pushed Marlene up to her floor and to the head nurse's station. On cue, Marlene jumped out of the chair. "Oh, my God!" the head nurse cried. "It's just like the Bible days!"

Hearing the commotion, a crowd of nurses appeared and began pushing Marlene from room to room so she could jump out of her wheelchair in front of all the other patients, who had become her friends. A minirevival broke out, and several patients became Christians on the spot.

Marlene's doctors could find no reason to detain her. After being interviewed by a forty-five-member panel of Mayo Clinic physicians, she was allowed to go home.

Marlene knew she could count on the merciful, compassionate, and loving God who had worked a miracle in her life. She decided to go to college, where she discovered she had a lot to learn.

"For instance," Marlene recalls, "you need to peel oranges before you eat them."

THE GOD OF MERCY, COMPASSION, AND LOVE

Marlene's experience with a loving, compassionate God aligns with Herbert Lockyer's portrayal of the miracles in Scripture. In his book *All the Miracles of the Bible,* Lockyer maintains that most of the miracles in the Bible were acts of mercy.[1] Marlene Klepees certainly recognized God's mercy, and she would also agree with another of Lockyer's assumptions. "Miracles," he wrote, "have a two-fold value, a physical and a spiritual."[2] Marlene experienced a physical healing, but equally important, she discovered God's heart. He loved her, accepted her, and promised to take care of her. It was more than anyone had ever offered— and by extending His mercy in this manner, the Lord healed Marlene's spirit.

A similar scene took place some two thousand years ago, when Jesus encountered a leper. In a remarkable display of boldness, the leper approached Jesus, saying, "Lord, if You are willing, You can make me clean."

For a leper to approach a clean person was almost unprecedented. A description of the disease, written in the nineteeth century, offers a telling picture: "Leprosy was nothing short of a living death, a corrupting of all the humours, a poisoning of the very springs of life; a dissolution little by little of the whole body, so that one limb after another actually decayed and fell away."[3] The Jews took leprosy to be an outward manifestation of inward sin, and people, including the rabbis, often threw stones at lepers as much as they would a mangy dog, to keep it away.[4]

Imagine how the leper must have felt as he approached the Lord. He was shunned and hated by others, and in keeping with Jewish law, he knew he was unclean and considered a dead man. No one was allowed to touch or speak to him. Nobody loved him—and he certainly did not love himself. How could he expect God to feel any differently?

In Christ, wrote Trench, love goes hand in hand with power.[5] When Jesus saw the leper, His heart filled with compassion and love. He did what no one else would have dared to do: He reached out and touched the man. "I am willing," He said. "Be cleansed."

Immediately the man was cured of his leprosy.[6]

Jesus did not see the leper as infectious or unclean. Instead, as Jamie Buckingham said, He saw him as God saw him—a human soul in desperate need.[7] And in His infinite mercy, the Lord imparted a spiritual restoration as well as a physical healing. The leprosy disappeared, but it was Christ's *touch*, rather than His verbal command, that communicated His love and acceptance. No one had ever touched the leper before.

The significance of this passage was not lost on Saint Francis, who ordered the brothers who served under him to minister to lepers for the love of Christ. It happened that the brothers worked in a hospital for lepers and other sick people. One leper was particularly difficult to care for; he abused all who tried to help him, shouting obscenities and physically striking any who came near. In the end the brethren decided the loathsome fellow must be possessed by the devil, and they left him to his own devices.

When the matter was reported to Saint Francis, he came to see the leper. "God give you peace, my dearest brother," Saint Francis said.

"And what peace could I get from God," the man spat angrily, "who has taken my peace and all I had from me, and made me rot and stink?"

Saint Francis urged the man to have patience and to endure his infirmity. "How?" the leper asked. "I am not only afflicted by my infirmity, but even worse by the friars you gave me to look after me, who do not tend me as they should."

Saint Francis began to pray for the man, and when he finished, he told the leper he would personally tend to his needs. "I will do whatever you wish," Saint Francis offered.

"I want you to wash me all over, for I stink so that I cannot bear myself."

Asking for a basin of hot water, Saint Francis undressed the man and began washing him with his own hands. Wherever Saint Francis touched him, the leprosy vanished and healthy flesh appeared in its place. Watching this miracle, the leper began to weep bitterly in repentance for his sins. "Woe unto me," he cried, "for I am worthy of hell for the insults and injuries I have given the brothers, and for the impatience and blasphemy I have offered to God!" He then made a general confession to a priest and received God's mercy.[8]

Saint Francis's leper, like the man Christ healed and like Marlene Klepees, received a double blessing from his miracle. His flesh was restored even as he received salvation. Like the others, he too saw a God of mercy, compassion, and love.

THE MAN WITH THE WITHERED LEG

Forrest Beiser, the young evangelist we met in chapter 8, can attest to God's loving compassion and power. Forrest completed his mission in Sri Lanka and went on to seminary. Upon graduation, he traveled to Zambia, where he played the organ at crusades held by the well-known evangelist Reinhard Bonnke. Bonnke liked to categorize each evening's service under a different label. They'd have "Deaf Persons Night," "Youth Night," and so on. The dynamic evangelist would inevitably preach a salvation message, but his prayer ministry tended to focus on a particular group of people singled out by the evening's theme.

During one crusade, the tent they were using proved too small to hold the ten thousand attendees, so the Bonnke team moved to a stadium that could accommodate the crowd. It was "Blind Persons Night." Everywhere he looked Forrest could see parents bringing children, and young adults leading the aged. Many of the afflicted had been blind from birth. It seemed that as Bonnke prayed, all of them were healed.

Unable to contain his curiosity, Forrest left his post at the organ and eased forward for a better view. Suddenly he spotted someone he recognized. Charles was an attractive boy of about fifteen. Forrest had met him on the first night of the crusade and immediately appreciated the teen's open, engaging smile. His demeanor was all the more unusual when Forrest considered that Charles had only one leg. The other was wasted away, shriveled inside the shorts he wore. As Charles hobbled around on a branch he used for a crutch, people could not help but notice his dangling limb.

Forrest liked the boy. He had to admit, however, that Charles made a somewhat gruesome picture. Moreover, he hated to think about it, but Forrest knew there was little hope for Charles's future. In a developing nation like his, disabled people could contribute little, and society did not waste time or attention on "cripples."

Forrest remembered the miracle he had witnessed in Sri Lanka, where God instantly healed a blind man's eyes. "God can heal your leg," he confided to Charles.

"Oh, no," Charles replied. "Last night was Lame Persons Night. I came, but nothing happened. God is not going to heal my leg."

"Charles," Forrest said, "God wants you to know His compassion."

As the rest of the crowd focused on the ministry going on near Bonnke's platform, Forrest quietly began to pray for his young friend. Nothing happened.

He was about to concede that perhaps Charles had been right when, strangely, Forrest felt impressed to smack the boy's leg and cry, "Be healed!"

To Forrest, the very idea was repugnant. He had been to seminary and was an intelligent, thoughtful adult. He had heard stories about flashy, showboat evangelists—and he certainly was not one of them. *I am not a goiter grabber!* he inwardly hissed to the Lord.

Nonetheless, the feeling persisted. Reasoning that he had nothing to lose, Forrest obeyed his impulse. He smacked Charles's withered leg. "Be healed, Charles!" he commanded.

Charles stiffened. Hit by the same power he had experienced in Sri Lanka, Forrest fainted again—marking the second time he had ever done such a thing.

Forrest saw Charles the following day. The teenager's leg was perfect and whole, allowing him to walk like any normal person. Touched by the compassionate power of God, Charles had become a whole man, inside and out.

Charles grew up, and with the help of another missionary, he became a teacher. In addition to illustrating God's compassion and sensitivity to our physical, spiritual, and emotional needs, Charles's story points to another aspect of God's character and power: God is sovereign. He works miracles when and where He wills. The Bonnke team had, for organizational and promotional purposes, established specific themes to attract specific people. But God was bigger than that. Charles, crippled since birth, received his healing on Blind Persons Night.

In the coming chapter, you will meet further evidences of God's sovereignty. Henry David Thoreau said, "People talk about Bible miracles because there is no miracle in their lives. Cease to gnaw that crust. There is ripe fruit over your head."[9]

There may be ripe fruit over your head. Only God knows, however, when it will fall.

CHAPTER 11

The Sovereign God

The hand of God is on every person and thing,
over-ruling all as it seemeth him good.

—JOHN WESLEY

OBERT SCOTT SHOOK HIS HEAD and tried to concentrate on the road before him. His hands gripped the steering wheel tighter and tighter as he willed himself to stay awake. He was exhausted—and it was only nine o'clock in the morning.

"Honey, are you okay?" his wife, Robin, asked.

Robert looked across the seat at his wife and managed a smile. "I guess I'll make it," he said.

Robert had eaten a rare bowl of oatmeal for breakfast. He knew the chances of his stomach being able to easily digest something so heavy were slim, but he had been hungry—and after all, it wasn't as though he were packing away a plateful of bacon and eggs. It was just a simple bowl of oatmeal.

Now, as he drove, Robert regretted his choice. His stomach was hurting, and in the supreme effort it took for his body to digest his breakfast, Robert felt all of his energy draining away. His grandfather had suffered from bleeding ulcers, and his uncle had had to have a third of his stomach removed. How long would

128

it be, Robert wondered, before he wound up in a condition like that?

Robert's mind wandered back to high school, when all the trouble began. His brother had been killed when his motorcycle collided with an oncoming car. Robert had taken the news hard. He could still see his brother's smiling face, heading off on his bike with his trademark casual wave.

After the accident, Robert had developed stomach problems. A battery of X rays and other tests revealed a preulceric condition his doctors feared would only worsen. Robert smiled wryly to himself. His family had never put much stock in medical opinion, but this time the doctor's predictions had been right on the mark.

That was more than twenty years ago. In the years since, Robert had successfully pursued a challenging doctorate in mass communications—thanks, in large part, to a seemingly endless intake of Maalox and other—stronger— prescription medicines. Next, he had accepted a teaching position at Asbury College in Kentucky, where the pressures of academia had increased his discomfort and reduced his diet to vegetables and nonacidic fruits. Now, living in Virginia, Robert realized the pain in his stomach seemed as natural as breathing. He supposed he would live this way forever, eating vegetables and drinking Maalox. Worse things could happen to a person.

Robert pulled his car into the parking lot of the church where he and his wife, Robin, had been going since their arrival in Virginia. They liked the minister; he taught with intelligence and a commitment to scriptural accuracy, and his messages always seemed relevant for today. Until now Robert had heard mostly dull sermons preached by men who, he felt, honestly believed the closer you got to sleep, the closer you drew to God. Robert had seen more than one pious head nod devoutly off in those services.

Sitting beside Robin as the service began, Robert tapped his foot in time with the music. His mind skipped ahead through the service. There would be, he knew, a time of prayer at the end—and the ever-present "altar call." Through the years Robert had responded to more of those calls than he cared to count. "They were on the twentieth verse of Just as I Am,'" he would explain to Robin. "If you don't go forward, they just keep singing. I didn't want to be the one person who wouldn't let everybody go home."

This time Robert resolved to stay in his seat. After all, he figured, nothing ever actually happened to the folks who went forward. Robert had never seen anybody get healed—although he had heard plenty of stories. But those were just fabrications, or psychosomatic "cures." There was always a logical explanation, Robert knew. His academic experience had confirmed what the church had taught him as a child: The miraculous gifts ended with the death of the last apostle.

As the service drew to a close, Robert joined the congregation in song. When the expected invitation came, he was prepared to leave quietly—but Robin held his arm.

"I want to go forward for prayer," she whispered. "I feel like I need it."

Robert could not argue. Money was tight, and he knew the pressure had taken its toll on both of them. Deciding to humor his wife, he guided her to the front of the church, where a throng of people already waited. He carefully positioned himself behind her, where he hoped he wouldn't be noticed.

Uh-oh. Robert looked to his left. The pastor—the man he and Robin so admired—was working the crowd, moving farther and farther away from Robert and Robin as he prayed his way down the line. In his place came another man, one Robert had never really liked. Unless he wanted to be prayed for by this eager fellow, Robert knew he had better make a move quickly.

He looked up and saw a door on his right marked exit. As discreetly as possible, Robert began inching Robin toward the door. *Only a few more steps, and then we're free,* he thought.

Suddenly, Robert felt a nudge. He turned and realized he was no longer behind his wife. A third man had intercepted them and was putting his hand on Robin's head. Robert hardly had time to contemplate the awkwardness of it all before he felt a hand on his own head. The same man who had prayed for Robin was praying for him—and the next thing Robert knew, he was out like a light.

When he came to, Robert felt a sensation in his abdomen. His stomach was contracting, and the spasms were clearly visible—although, to Robert's relief, no one really seemed to be watching.

"I look like I'm having a baby," Robert hissed to his wife. He realized he ought to be embarrassed. But even as he spoke, he felt a calming peace flow through his body, and he lost all track of time.

After a while, he and Robin found a couple of chairs. Almost everyone had left the service, and Robert reckoned it was finally appropriate to go home. "I don't know what happened back there," he said to himself as much as to Robin as the two of them climbed into their car.

It was two days before Robert realized he could not feel his stomach. He had overslept, and without time for a light breakfast before he drove Robin to work, he braced himself for the pain he knew was sure to come. Never had he been able to function on an empty stomach; the ulcers were always a sharp reminder to eat.

"Robin," Robert said hesitantly, "I can't feel anything. I know that sounds strange. But I've lived with this stomach pain every day for more than ten years—and now it's gone."

"Maybe you've been healed," Robin suggested.

Robert's mind was not ready to accept that. Instead, he decided to run a few tests.

The next morning he again skipped breakfast—and waited for the consequences. Nothing. Convinced now that something had happened, he drove to the nearest Taco Bell. He gobbled the spicy Mexican food. Still nothing.

Finally, Robert took Robin out to dinner on Saturday night and did something he hadn't done in more than a decade. He ordered a steak—and he relished every last bite.

"It seems," he finally conceded, "that I have been healed."

Robert had not been looking for a miracle. He had gone forward for prayer simply to oblige his wife, not to ask God for a healing. And yet God, in His sovereignty, chose that moment to reach down and touch him—even though Robert had neither the expectation nor even the faith to believe for a miracle.

THE MISSING MOTIVE

In his book *Surprised by the Power of the Spirit,* Jack Deere describes an instance where he prayed for an unborn baby girl after a sonogram showed that one of her kidneys had shriveled and would not function normally. Ten days later a second sonogram revealed both of her kidneys were the same size and perfectly normal.[1]

Deere admits, however, that on other occasions he has prayed for babies who were ultimately miscarried or stillborn. Why would God respond to one prayer and not another? Why would He heal Robert Scott—a fellow who did not even really believe miracles still happen?

I like the way Deere handles questions like these. "Today," he wrote, "there are times when the Lord heals someone that we would never have expected him to heal, or he does it in a way we would not expect. Conversely, there are times when we would expect him to heal and he doesn't, and again he gives no reasons for it. All of this points to the fact that God truly is sovereign and that he does not reveal all of his purposes to us."[2]

This pattern finds precedent in a number of the miracles Christ performed. In one instance, for example, He came upon an invalid who was lying beside the pool of Bethesda. Bethesda was a magnet for sick people—the blind, lame, and paralyzed lay about the pool, and when the water began to bubble or stir, those who could get into the pool before the motion stopped were healed.

When Jesus saw the helpless man He asked, "Do you want to be made well?"

"Sir," the fellow replied, "I have no man to put me into the pool when the water is stirred up; but while I am coming, another steps down before me."

Then Jesus said to him, "Rise, take up your bed and walk."

Immediately, the Bible says, the man was cured; he picked up his mat and left.[3]

Why, when Jesus was obviously surrounded by people who were desperate for miracles, did He single out that one man for healing? Why did He even stop to speak to him? No mention is made of the fellow's faith. Moreover, he had been lying there for thirty-eight years; obviously, Jesus did not heal him to remove any obstacles to the man's ministry or meet any of his immediate needs. For the invalid, lying beside the pool had become a way of life.

Reading the passage in the Bible, there is no evidence that the fellow ever prayed for a healing. When the miracle happened, it did not draw people to Christ; on the contrary, it served to incite the Jewish leaders to anger and got them plotting as to how they might do away with Jesus. The healing may have been an awesome feat, but people were more concerned with the fact that Jesus healed on the Sabbath than with this tangible demonstration of God's power.

Finally, there is no reference to Christ's compassion or His love for the fellow. Instead, Jesus follows the healing with a warning: "Sin no more, lest a worse thing come upon you." Obviously Christ loved the man, but that was not, apparently, the motive behind the miracle.

We do not know why Christ healed the invalid that day. Likewise, we cannot explain why He did not continue to let His power flow and clear the poolside in an afternoon. Herbert Lockyer offers as plausible an answer as I've heard: "Because of all God is in Himself, and all He possesses, He has unlimited freedom to accomplish what He deems best."[4]

THE GIRL WHO WAS BORN WITHOUT PUPILS

A classic example of God's exercising His freedom to do as He thinks best is the story of Gemma di Giordi, a young girl born with double papillary atrophy—in layman's terms, born without pupils. Her doctors considered it impossible that she should ever see.

Gemma's eyes were two black spots, incapable of movement. Frequent spasmodic convulsions in her eyelids only emphasized the problem. Even so, Gemma's grandmother refused to give up hope. She had heard about Padre Pio and his remarkable healing ministry. With her seven-year-old granddaughter in tow, she set off to find the priest.

When they arrived in Padre Pio's town, he was celebrating Mass. Gemma and her grandmother attended the service, and afterward, the priest beckoned to them. "You want to make your first Communion, isn't that so, Gemma?" he asked.

With no mention of her desire for a miracle, Gemma made her confession and received her first Communion. When they finished Padre Pio bestowed a simple blessing: "May our Lady bless you, Gemma. Be a good girl."

Be a good girl! What kind of a mighty proclamation was that? Gemma's grandmother might have been tempted to ask for something more substantial, but before she could even think, Gemma let out a cry.

"I can see!" the child said, looking into Padre Pio's kind and smiling face. Without asking for a miracle or even mentioning her need, Gemma was cured.

Later, when an eye specialist examined the little girl, he found that she still had no pupils. The doctor confessed that Gemma exhibited a continued and permanent intervention of the supernatural, since, without pupils, it is naturally impossible to see.[5] In the mystery of this story lies the primary purpose of miracles.

They may have many contributing factors—such as faith, prayer, and the compassion of Christ—but they all are designed with one goal in mind: *All miracles serve to bring glory to God.*

Few stories testify to God's sovereignty as well as His glory as poignantly as Duane Miller's miracle. I first heard the story on a "Focus on the Family" broadcast, where it brought tears to my eyes and sent a tingle up my spine. It's a miracle that is better heard than read about, but after talking with Duane and considering his experience, I had to try to recount his story here.

"YOU CAN'T PUT GOD IN A BOX"

Duane Miller began singing professionally when he was only sixteen years old, touring the country with a gospel quartet. Thus, when he became a pastor, it seemed perfectly natural for him to incorporate a song into his sermon or build his sermon around the message in a song. He had arranged just such a presentation on the morning his ordeal began.

Duane woke up with the flu. It wasn't full-blown yet, but he could feel all the symptoms coming on, including a scratchy throat that already threatened to be nasty. Wearily he dressed for church, determined to make the best of the situation. He had planned to sing "Jesus, Just the Mention of Your Name" as part of his sermon on the Lord's name.

He made it through the early service, but by the time the congregation filed in for the eleven o'clock service, Duane's voice was shot. He dispensed with the song and labored through the sermon. When he finished, he went home and crawled into bed.

Duane battled the flu for ten days. Finally all of the symptoms disappeared—except that his throat was still sore and he sounded as though he had an awful case of laryngitis. Desperate for relief, he consulted a specialist.

The doctor peered into Duane's throat. "I don't know how you can even breathe—there is so much infection and your throat is so swollen," he said. "I am going to give you some medication to reduce the swelling."

With the medicine, the swelling disappeared, as did the soreness in Duane's throat. His voice, however, did not return, and Duane consulted a team of doctors at Houston's Baylor College of Medicine. Unable to pinpoint the problem, the doctors surmised that it might be stress-related, and they encouraged Duane to take a six-month sabbatical from his ministerial duties.

Duane obliged, but after half a year, his voice was no stronger. He knew he could not ask his church to keep him on as their senior pastor, and he resigned.

As Duane continued speaking in a hoarse croak, relying on the fatty "false chords" in his throat, his doctors ruled out the possibilities, one after the other. He did not have cancer, epilepsy, or multiple sclerosis. Finally, they concluded that a virus must have penetrated the myelin sheath that surrounded his vocal chords, damaging the nerves. The damage was permanent; Duane would never regain the use of his vocal chords. Moreover, he could expect to lose what little voice he had as he wore away at the fatty lobes that served as his makeshift voice box.

Duane realized he would never be able to preach again. Even more discouraging was the knowledge that he could no longer sing. What, Duane wondered, would he do? Beyond the frustration of his physical limitations was the inescapable reality that he had a family to support. His daughters were in college. How would he survive?

Eventually Duane landed a job doing title research as a private investigator for the legal department of a federal agency. The work required little spoken communication, and Duane settled into the job. Then, as suddenly as it had started, the work stopped. His employers quit calling. "We're reorganizing," they said. "We'll get back to you."

Next, Duane's insurance carrier dropped his coverage when they discovered that the doctors had given him no expected time line for recovery. "With no clear cure, your medical treatment falls under the 'experimental' category—and we don't cover that," the carrier explained.

At about the same time, Duane's disability income dried up. Since he was not completely disabled, he no longer qualified for the benefits.

Mustering his resolve, Duane decided to try writing—a talent he suspected he had but had never had the time to pursue. He put together a book proposal and sent it to two publishers. He received replies from both of them on the same day, a Friday. Sinking into his chair in the living room, Duane tore open the letters. They were almost identical: *We like your idea,* the letters read, *but since you have no name recognition we would have to put you on a speaking tour to ensure strong sales for the book. Without your voice you could not promote the book. We're very sorry.*

Contemplating the rejections, Duane heard the telephone ring. "Hello?" he said.

A friend from his old legal employer was on the line. "I wanted to explain why we stopped hiring you," he said. "I'm embarrassed to be calling, but I think you deserve an explanation. Our lawyers were worried that they might have to put you on the witness stand at some point and that your voice might be a problem with the jurors."

Duane could hardly believe his ears. He had no insurance, no income, no book contracts, and no job—all because of his wretched, raspy voice. "God," he cried, "I just don't see the point anymore. I have nothing left to give."

The glimmer of light in Duane's dark world came from his former Sunday school class. Knowing he needed an outlet and respecting his ability as a teacher, the Sunday school invited him to teach the two-hundred-member group. Duane did not want to subject them to the sound of his voice, but the class pressed him to accept the offer.

On Sunday—two days after the publishers' rejections had plunged Duane into despair—he opened his notes and began teaching from the standard Southern Baptist curriculum, one that had been set some six years earlier. Relying on special microphones, amplification equipment, and the patience of his listeners, Duane asked the class to turn to the Psalms.

The lesson began with Psalm 68, a song of praise remembering the deeds of the Lord. When God led the Israelites in the wilderness, Duane explained, He had a plan. They might have been going in circles, but they were following God. "When God moved, it was with a purpose," Duane said. "He hasn't changed. That's still true."

Next, still speaking in his raspy voice, Duane directed the class to Psalm 103—the second part of the morning's preselected lesson. "It says God forgives all my sins," Duane croaked into the microphone. "His grace gives us things we don't deserve."

Duane read the next part of the verse: *"He heals all my diseases."*

"You can't put God in a box," Duane explained. "I believe God still heals. God heals in His sovereign will. I don't know why God does things He does, but I know He does, and the only thing He requires of me is to allow Him to be God and me to be me.

"To say that every single person will always be healed because Jesus died on the cross is a misinterpretation of Scripture," Duane continued. "On the other hand, to say that because we do not have anything after the book of Acts, that miracles ended with the book of Acts and never happened again, is equally wrong. Either way, you're putting God into a box. And He doesn't want to be in a box."

Duane moved through the psalm. *"He redeems my life from the pit."* Thinking of his despair just two days earlier, Duane could not help but smile. "I like that verse," he said. "I have had and you have had, in times past, pit experiences. We've all had times when our lives seemed to be in a pit, in a grave..."

Duane paused. He had felt something give way in his throat when he said the word pit. Had the class sensed it? He decided to keep speaking.

"...and we didn't have an answer for the pit we found ourselves in."

Now there was no question. Duane's voice had suddenly, miraculously, returned. It had grown stronger and more confident with each word. The Sunday school class, awed at first, began to laugh, cry, and clap sporadically. Had they—could they have—just witnessed a miracle?

"I don't understand this right now," Duane said, his clear voice coming through the microphone. "I'm overwhelmed. It sounds funny to say, but I'm at a loss for words."

With that, the crowd erupted. Two hundred people had seen a miracle and—even better—they had it all on tape because their class routinely recorded the lesson. Searching for words to describe his emotions, Duane quoted a song by Andre Crouch: "How can I say thanks for all the things that you've done for me; Things so undeserved, and yet you came to prove your love for me. The voices of a million angels could not express my gratitude." Duane's voice trailed off. "It's been three years to the day since I preached my last sermon," he said, choking back a sob. "God never does anything without a purpose...Oh! This is *fun!*"

Duane was not expecting a miracle. Looking back, he believes God sovereignly healed him where and when He did to provide encouragement—to him and to others. For the Sunday school class and for the countless people who have since heard the tape that documented his healing, Duane says God has a message. "God cares about you, just as He cares about me. You may think that He has lost your address, but He knows exactly what's going on in your life."

This message—that God knows and cares about our lives—is the cornerstone of this book. His miracles, like His grace, represent an unmerited expression of divine love for mortal men.

How we respond to this expression is up to us.
Do we want to know God's love?
Are we willing to experience a miracle?

Expect a Miracle

ERHAPS, WHEN YOU FIRST PICKED UP THIS BOOK, you did not believe in miracles. Maybe you thought they were possible—at least in Bible times—but you did not seriously consider that they might happen today. Or maybe you knew that God still works miracles, but only in certain circumstances, and only for other people.

On the other hand, maybe you fully expect God to work miracles anytime, anywhere. Peter Wagner, a professor of church growth at Fuller Theological Seminary, points to an explosion of miracles taking place in some churches today. "We live in an exceptional time," he says. "In the Middle Ages in Europe, perhaps, there may have been something comparable. But certainly in the history of the U.S. we have never seen such a frequency of signs and wonders."[1]

Even with these evidences, though, it is one thing to say you believe in miracles—and quite another to ask God to perform one. *Is it okay to ask God for a miracle?*

I believe God wants us to ask Him for miracles—provided we ask with right motives. Jesus never rebuked anyone who came to Him in faith or in need seeking healing, deliverance, or some other kind of miracle.[2] Instead, Christ actually commanded His disciples to anticipate miracles, telling them to go out and "Heal the sick, cleanse the lepers, raise the dead, cast out demons."[3] When we ask God for miracles with the right motives, we are, in fact, responding to His command.

God is sovereign; we cannot put Him into a box. Some modern thinkers, however, will try. They will put God in a box and fasten the lid, saying miracles happen only seldom, if at all. But the testimony of biblical, historical, and contemporary experience proves these people wrong. Miracles happen.

Today, when you come upon serious needs in people's lives, do not be afraid to ask God to intervene. As the examples in this book illustrate, He is willing and able to use miracles to build our faith, overcome the obstacles we face, meet our needs, answer our prayers, and confirm His message of love for us.

Above all, God is willing to work miracles to glorify Himself. He wants us to know Him in all of His glory. When we behold a miracle, when we suddenly recognize God's power and His love, God wants us to have no choice but to respond as Thomas did, when he beheld the resurrected Christ: "My Lord and my God!"

~ Notes ~

Chapter 1: *When God Comes Down*

1. Gallup/*USA Today*/CNN Poll, cited in the *Providence Journal Bulletin*, 28 January 1995.
2. Eph. 3:20–21 (NIV).
3. R. A. Brown, H. Rode, A. J. W. Millar, et al., "Colorectal Carcinoma in Children," *Journal of Pediatric Surgery* 27 (1992): 919–21.
4. Definition cited by Herbert Lockyer in *All the Miracles of the Bible* (Grand Rapids, Mich.: Zondervan, 1961), 13.
5. C. S. Lewis, *Miracles* (New York: Macmillan, 1947, 1960), 5.
6. Lockyer, *All the Miracles of the Bible*, 13.
7. Oswald Chambers, *My Utmost for His Highest* (New York: Dodd, Mead & Company, 1935), 25.
8. Ralph M. McInerny, *Miracles: A Catholic View* (Huntington, Ind.: Our Sunday Visitor, 1986), 13.
9. Norman L. Geisler and Ronald M. Brooks, *When Skeptics Ask* (Wheaton, Ill.: Victor, 1990), 82.
10. McInerny, *Miracles: A Catholic View*, 14.
11. See Acts 8:9–20.
12. Geisler and Brooks, *When Skeptics Ask*, 88.
13. Lockyer, *All the Miracles of the Bible*, 17.
14. See Exod. 7:6–8:19.
15. R. C. Trench, *Notes on the Miracles of Our Lord* (Grand Rapids, Mich.: Baker, 1949), 15–16.

16. Lewis, *Miracles*, 132.

Chapter 2: *A Case for Modern Miracles*

1. Jack Deere, *Surprised by the Power of the Spirit* (Grand Rapids, Mich.: Zondervan, 1993), 54.
2. Malcolm Muggeridge, *Jesus Rediscovered* (Garden City, N.Y.: Doubleday, 1969), 175.
3. Ibid., 109.
4. Jean Hellé, *Miracles* (New York: David McKay, 1952), 93.
5. Ibid., 85.
6. Ibid., 231–33.
7. Jamie Buckingham, *Miracle Power* (Ann Arbor, Mich.: Servant, 1988, 1990), v–vi.
8. Ibid., viii–x.
9. Lewis, *Miracles*, 81.
10. Luke 8:53.
11. John 20:24–29.
12. Benedicta Ward, *Miracles and the Medieval Mind* (Philadelphia: University of Pennsylvania Press, 1982), 30.
13. Geisler and Brooks, *When Skeptics Ask*, 75.
14. See 2 Kings 5:1–15.
15. Heb. 13:8.
16. Jamie Buckingham, *Daughter of Destiny* (Plainfield, N.J.: Logos International, 1976), 215.
17. Lewis, *Miracles*, 94.

Chapter 3: *Prayer Matters*

1. Catherine Marshall, *The Helper* (New York: Avon, 1978), 114.
2. Ibid., 115.

3. Chambers, *My Utmost for His Highest,* 348.
4. Deere, *Surprised by the Power of the Spirit,* 166.
5. Elisabeth Jay, ed., *The Journals of John Wesley* (Oxford: Oxford University Press, 1987), jacket copy.
6. Ibid., 59.
7. Ibid., 86–87.
8. This story about another missionary was told by OC International missionaries Keith and Charlotte Brown in November 1991, Colorado Springs, Colorado.
9. Marshall, *The Helper,* 116.
10. Deere, *Surprised by the Power of the Spirit,* 164.
11. Luke 8:50.
12. Luke 8:53–55.
13. Marshall, *The Helper,* 157.
14. Annie Dillard, cited by Guy Chevreau in *Catch the Fire: The Toronto Blessing* (Toronto: HarperCollins, 1994), 2.
15. Geisler and Brooks, *When Skeptics Ask,* 82.
16. Marshall, *The Helper,* 156.

Chapter 4: *The Faith Factor*

1. Lockyer, *All the Miracles of the Bible,* 175.
2. See Matt. 15:21–28.
3. Trench, *Notes on the Miracles of Our Lord,* 217.
4. See Rom. 10:17.

Chapter 5: *Overcoming Obstacles*

1. Matt. 8:14–15.
2. John 11:25–26.

3. Ward, *Miracles and the Medieval Mind,* 2.
4. Ibid., 101.
5. Edwin Abbott, *St. Thomas of Canterbury* (London: Adam and Charles Black, 1898), 227.
6. Ibid., 223.
7. Ibid., 225.
8. Ibid., 240–41.
9. See 1 Cor. 12:7; 14:12, 26.

Chapter 6: *Help Is on the Way*

1. Elisabeth Elliot, *A Lamp for My Feet* (Ann Arbor, Mich.: Vine Books, 1985), 96.
   2. Num. 20:2–11.
3. Hellé, *Miracles,* 82.
4. Ruth Cranston, *The Miracle of Lourdes* (New York: McGraw-Hill, 1955), 13–15.
5. Buckingham, *Miracle Power,* 9.
6. Trench, *Notes on the Miracles of Our Lord,* 10.
7. Ibid., 11.

Chapter 7: *Answered Prayer*

1. Wayne Grudem, *Systematic Theology: An Introduction to Biblical Doctrine* (Leicester, England: IV Press; Grand Rapids, Mich.: Zondervan, 1994), 357.
2. See 1 Kings 17:17–24; Mark 7:32–35; Acts 12:1–14.
3. Grudem, *Systematic Theology,* 358.
4. See 2 Chron. 16:12–13.
5. Nancy Gibbs, "The Message of Miracles," *Time* magazine, 10 April 1995, 72.

Chapter 8: *God's Stamp of Approval*

1. Mark 16:20.
2. Acts 14:3.

3. John 14:11.
4. See Acts 9:33–35.
5. See Acts 9:36–42.
6. John 3:2.
7. See Exod. 4:1–9.
8. Num. 12:3.
9. Friedrich Heer, *The Medieval World*, cited by Lawrence Cunningham in *St. Francis of Assisi* (San Francisco: Harper & Row, 1981), 39.
10. Omer Englebert, *St. Francis of Assisi: A Biography* (Chicago: Franciscan Herald Press) 310.
11. Morris Bishop, *St. Francis of Assisi* (Boston: Little, Brown and Company, 1974), 168.
12. Englebert, *St. Francis of Assisi*, 310–11.
13. Hilda C. Graef, *The Case of Therese Neumann* (Westminster, Md.: Newman Press, 1951), 27.
14. Bishop, *St. Francis of Assisi*, 172.
15. Ibid., 168.

Chapter 9: *That's Awesome!*

1. John 14:29.
2. Isaiah 55:10.
3. Augustine, cited in Ward, *Miracles and the Medieval Mind*, 2.
4. Grudem, *Systematic Theology*, 355.
5. Gibbs, "The Message of Miracles," 68.
6. Deere, *Surprised by the Power of the Spirit*, 223.
7. Lockyer, *All the Miracles of the Bible*, 14.
8. Malachy Carroll and Pol de Leon Albert, *Three Studies in Simplicity* (Chicago: Franciscan Herald Press, 1974), 35.

9. Ibid., 36.
10. Ibid., 36–37.
11. Dallas Plemmons, *Hell in the Land of the Morning Calm* (Virginia Beach, Va.: McDonough Media Publications Group, 1987), 119–28.

Chapter 10: *Heart-to-Heart*

1. Lockyer, *All the Miracles of the Bible*, 15.
2. Ibid.
3. Trench, *Notes on the Miracles of Our Lord*, 134.
4. Buckingham, *Miracle Power*, 143.
5. Trench, *Notes on the Miracles of Our Lord*, 136.
6. See Matt. 8:1–3.
7. Buckingham, *Miracle Power*, 147.
8. Otto Karrer, ed., *St. Francis of Assisi: The Legends and Lauds* (London: Sheed & Ward, 1947), 208–9.
9. Gibbs, "The Message of Miracles," 73.

Chapter 11: *The Sovereign God*

1. Deere, *Surprised by the Power of the Spirit*, 127–28.
2. Ibid., 227.
3. See John 5:1–9.
4. Lockyer, *All the Miracles of the Bible*, 22.
5. Carroll and Albaret, *Three Studies in Simplicity*, 53–55.

Epilogue: *Expect a Miracle*

1. Gibbs, "The Message of Miracles," 68.
2. Grudem, *Systematic Theology*, 370.
3. Matt. 10:8.